Practicing the Art of Shut the Hell Up!

A Modern Guide to Shutting Up, Showing Up, and Leading with Emotional Clarity

Practicing the Art of Shut the Hell Up!

A Modern Guide to
Shutting Up, Showing Up, and
Leading with Emotional Clarity

Corrie Zimerla

ISBN: 978-1-970615-01-2

Piper Publishing
3576 West 159th St.
Cleveland, OH 44111
www.piper-publishing.com

Cover Design by Jim MacLeod
Interior Design by Marc Maxhimer

Table of Contents

Preface / A Light in the Dark

My journey around the sun so far has definitely taken the scenic route. It was not a straight line—it was more like an obstacle course wrapped in chaos with plenty of detours, a few collisions, and some long, silent stretches I was not sure I would make it through. But here I am. And for the first time, with a grounded, rooted kind of certainty, I can say: I am standing in my purpose.

That kind of clarity does not arrive gently. It is forged. Pressed out of the hardest seasons and refined in the fire of disappointment, heartbreak, and resilience. My map was hand-drawn in real time, in the margins of grief and hope, in moments no one clapped for. This path—spiraled as it has been—taught me how to walk by determination, not by sight. And somewhere along the way, I stopped needing to have all the answers. I just needed to stay aligned with my inner compass. This kind of quiet strength is not flashy. It does not wear a title or carry a megaphone. It listens more than it speaks. It makes room. It pays attention to the unspoken. It understands that real power is quiet, not because it is timid, but because it is secure.

In some ways, this book is a love letter to every life I've walked beside. The ones I have raised, the ones I have mentored, the ones I have served, the ones whose stories I still carry in my heart. And yes, to the souls I have had to release, too. Sometimes love means staying. Sometimes it means letting go. And both require courage and strength.

This turn of the wheel in my life is not about proving anything. It is about presence. About choosing softness in a world that prizes hardness. About walking gently in spaces that taught me to armor up. About showing up, heart-first, even when it would be easier to check out.

There is a gravity in that kind of responsibility. It makes every interaction feel significant. It turns everyday moments into sacred opportunities. And, if I am being honest, it takes daily practice. Every exchange becomes a chance to fine-tune the art of showing up, appreciation, kindness, and compassion. Not because it is easy—because it is necessary.

This is my framework for living. My mantra. My lens for every obstacle, redirection, and blessing I have encountered. It is not a one-size-fits-all blueprint—but it is mine. My recipe for a life well-lived and worth living.

More than anything, I hope this work becomes a quiet lantern—something others can carry forward on their own paths, even if our trails never cross. I hope to be remembered as a light in the dark. A safe haven for peace. A voice that whispers, calm waters are ahead. A steady harbor for those still battling their inner storms. I want people to walk away from our conversations feeling lighter—not because I have fixed anything, but because I have helped them remember the wholeness they already carry.

I have had the great privilege—and the wild, humbling honor—of crossing paths with some truly extraordinary humans. People whose mere existence reshaped the air in the room. Some taught with words, others simply by living fully in their truth. Their wisdom, both spoken and silent, has shaped me in ways I am still discovering. There are too many to name and even more I cannot remember clearly, but trust me—they are here. Their fingerprints are all over these pages. Their lessons echo between the lines, are stitched into the subtext, and tucked inside the rhythm of each sentence. Some brought grace, others grit. Some brought knives and left wounds. All imprinted something. What I carry forward is a messy, beautiful mosaic of their truths—filtered through my eyes, my heart, and my understanding.

Hail to the second moms, the teachers who saw potential before I did, the mentors who told the truth when it was hard, the bosses who led with integrity (or at the very least taught me what not to do), the colleagues who reminded me daily of our purpose—and served as sanity savers when surrounded by chaos, nonsense, or the occasional meeting that could have been an email—and the friends who sat with me in silence when there were no words. Thank you. You may not even know the impact you have had, but I carry your lessons (and your coping strategies) with me every single day.

I pride myself on the relationships I have built. Each one is meaningful in its own way, a constellation of connections that has shaped me. People are not problems to be solved—they are stories to be honored. And if I have learned anything in this lifetime, it is that healing rarely happens in isolation. It happens in deep connections. In being seen. In being witnessed while in sacred space.

I have learned that people do not always need solutions. They need sanctuary. They need someone who will not flinch at their truth, someone who will not shrink in the face of their shadow. They need to be believed. That is the kind of human I aim to be.

Most of what I know—what I *really* know—did not come from books or degrees or certifications. The most invaluable lessons revealed themselves in silence, in the spaces between the noise: how someone shifts in their chair. The tension of a jawline. The pause before someone answers, "I'm fine." It is there, in the subtle, quiet places, that truth lives.

My professional intention was never to collect titles. It has always been about creating less harm, more hope, and becoming a stronger version of myself along the way. From my earliest days as a nursing assistant to the mission-driven work in community health and medical research, every step was an act of service—and a lesson. Not just in competence, but in awareness. To listen. To hold space. To lead with heart.

My love language is safety; emotional safety. Physical safety. Psychological safety. The kind of safety that says: You can be your messy, rigid, beautifully contradictory self here.You do not have to perform. You do not have to shrink. Just breathe. I have you.

This is not about toxic positivity. This is about grounded hope. A hope that can sit in the dirt with you and say, "Even here, *especially* here, we are not alone."

I am fluent in silence.
I am here to remind you of your power.

Sometimes the most sacred gift you can offer someone is your steady existence and a simple reminder: You are not too much. You never were.

The further along this journey I go, the more I have realized how deeply sacred it is to witness someone else's healing. It is not always loud or dramatic. Often, it is quiet. Like the moment someone laughs again after forgetting how. When they finally say what they really mean without apology. When they stop explaining their worth and simply embody it. Those are the miracles I live for.

And maybe that is the whole point. To keep showing up, especially when no one is watching. To bring softness where there has been hardness. To offer truth without harm. To bring light into dark rooms—whether anyone notices or not. Maybe our legacy is not built in headlines but in heartbeats. In the thousand quiet ways we show others they matter.

So, if you are holding this book, I hope you find something in these pages that makes you feel a little more seen. A little less alone. Maybe even a little more whole. The world is noisy, messy, and often unkind. But I promise you—hope is everywhere, if you know where to look.

Let this be your reminder to be it.
Let this be your invitation to look for it.
Let this be the moment you choose to show up differently—not because the world changed, but because you did.

Foreword

By Philip A. Cola, PhD

I have spent more than three decades working at the intersections of psychology, medicine, and management, first as a psychiatric researcher, then as a biomedical research manager, later as a management scholar, and continuously as a practitioner navigating leadership, complex systems, and people in real time. Across those roles, one truth has remained remarkably consistent: success, health, and meaning rise or fall on the quality of our relationships, both with others and with ourselves.

In this foreword, I write not as the author of this book, but as a colleague, scholar, and practitioner reflecting on work that addresses a gap I have seen repeatedly across research, leadership, and lived experience.

That truth is not new. In fact, it is so widely accepted that it risks becoming background noise when you point it out. Some of my own research introduces the idea of "relational capacity," or the ability to develop deep and meaningful bi-directional relationships with others. Furthermore, entire libraries of books, articles, keynote talks, and training programs, some that I have used or delivered, tell us that strong interpersonal relationships matter. What we understand far less clearly is how to adopt and sustain these relational practices across complex professional and personal environments, especially as conditions change.

This gap often decreases performance and psychological safety while inhibiting further learning in the moment, leading to communication failures that undermine even the most technically competent groups or teams. We know these things empirically, intellectually, and often painfully through experience and through evidence-based management.

And yet, knowing is not the same as doing. Relationships in the real world are so complex that few of us have a reliable map for how to manage ourselves, or ourselves in relation to others, in a consistent way. There is simply too much variability across context and situation. Peter Drucker, the father of modern management thinking, tried to guide us through his essay on "Managing Oneself." However, that is only a starting point that often frustrates individuals due to the inherent complexity of the world. While foundational, that guidance is often insufficient for navigating the emotional and relational demands of modern life.

What most people struggle with is not whether relationships matter, but how to build them, how to sustain them under pressure, and how to remain grounded and coherent when relationships are strained by stress, power dynamics, competing incentives, or emotional overload. This is the gap where theory often stops and lived experience begins. It is precisely here that this book steps in.

I met Corrie Zimerla many years ago after conducting research on schizophrenia in the Department of Psychiatry at Case Western Reserve University, when I was leading the clinical research enterprise at the affiliated hospital of the same academic medical center. She was just beginning her career as a psychiatric researcher herself. That shared foundation in psychiatry immersed us both in the human realities of distress, identity, resilience, and the hope for growth and repair. Since then, our professional paths have evolved in different but complementary directions. I remained anchored in psychology and organizational behavior, eventually holding academic appointments in management and medicine. Corrie went on to become a director of operations for a clinical and academic department and later an associate dean at the same medical centers where our careers began. These journeys kept us squarely engaged with complex systems, institutional structures, and leadership decisions that shape people's daily working and personal lives.

What connects those trajectories is not coincidence; it is coherence. Both of us have spent our careers observing how systems affect people, how people respond to pressure, and how quickly even the most capable individuals can lose their footing when clarity, energy, or self-trust erodes. This work reflects those shared experiences. It carries the psychological depth of being a student of human behavior, the pragmatic realism of administrative leadership, and the reflective wisdom that only comes from trying, again and again, to support students, faculty, leaders, and patients at moments when performance alone was not enough to move forward.

This is not a book that tells you to "communicate better," "set boundaries," or "practice self-care" in the abstract. Those prescriptions are everywhere and are insufficient on their own. What distinguishes this book is its insistence on practice. She offers concrete steps for how to act, how to listen, how to regulate, how to choose, and how to recover across contexts that will feel familiar to anyone navigating modern professional and personal life.

Initially trained as a research psychologist, I am particularly struck by how she respects the fundamentals of human functioning and behavior. She understands that insight without regulation collapses under stress, that values without habits dissolve under fatigue, and that good intentions without structure rarely survive real-world complexity. As someone later trained in management and organizational behavior, I appreciate how clearly the book links individual practices to collective outcomes. It compellingly shows how small, daily choices shape behavior, culture, trust, and energy over time. As a practitioner-scholar of management, I have come to view these tools not as ideals, but as survival skills.

One of the book's central contributions is its reframing of habits, boundaries, and reflection as a framework for sustainable growth. Relationships do not thrive on inspiration alone; they require systems that support consistency, clarity, and repair. She treats emotional regulation, listening, self-loyalty, and values alignment not as personality traits but as skills that can be practiced, refined, and sustained. That distinction matters. It shifts responsibility away from "being better" and toward building better systems for being human. This will help us sustain the all-important relationships in life.

Equally important is the way the book invites the reader into active reflection. Each chapter does not merely explain; it pauses. It asks questions about surface patterns, reveals energy leaks, and prompts honest self-assessment. In my own teaching and research, I have found that reflection is the link between awareness and change. Without it, even the best advice becomes fleeting. With it, insight becomes something you can carry into meetings, conversations, conflicts, and decisions.

Corrie also does something increasingly rare: she refuses to separate professional competence from personal integrity. In an era where productivity is often prioritized over presence and performance metrics eclipse well-being, she argues, quietly but firmly, that sustainability is the true measure of success. Not the absence of difficulty, but the capacity to remain centered within it. Coherence rather than perfection.

I have watched leaders burn out not because they lacked intelligence or dedication, but because they lacked daily practices that protected their energy, sharpened their decision-making, and reminded them who they were becoming. She offers those practices. Not as rigidity, but as resilience. Not as withdrawal, but as grounded engagement.

If you are looking for a simple route, this is not it. If you are looking for a shortcut, you will not find one here. What you will find instead is something far more valuable: a practical, humane guide to building relationships that endure—through how you speak, how you listen, how you choose, and how you show up when it would be easier to react or retreat.

This book matters because it meets people where they actually live, in the space between intention and action, insight and exhaustion, connection and overwhelm. It acknowledges the noise of modern life without surrendering to it. It offers guidance on small, repeatable practices that, over time, change how you experience yourself and others.

As someone who has devoted a career to understanding human behavior in complex systems, I can say with confidence that this work is both timely and timeless. It is grounded without being heavy,

reflective without being indulgent, and practical without being re-
ductive. Most importantly, it respects the agency of the reader. It
does not tell you who to be. It shows you how to build the conditions
that allow your best self to emerge, consistently, sustainably, and in
relation with others.

That is rare, and it is worth your attention. Enjoy.

Philip A. Cola, PhD
Professor of Management and Medicine
Case Western Reserve University
January 2026

Introduction

No, It Is Not Just About Being Nice (or Smart)

The truth most people avoid is that being smart is not enough. Intelligence alone does not build healthy relationships, cohesive teams, or sustainable environments—and we have all met brilliant minds who collapse in tough conversations, turning them into awkward monologues. Intelligence without emotional grounding is all flair, no foundation. It may look impressive on paper, but in real life, it rarely holds.

And nice? Nice is a shrug. Forgettable. It is the free trial version of human connection. What people actually need is depth—approachable, trustworthy, emotionally anchored. Because when the metaphorical (or literal) fan gets hit, no one cares if you are nice. They care if you are steady enough to stay grounded, clear enough to be understood, and strong enough to sit in discomfort without making it worse.

This is not about being an eternal optimist or the empath who cries at animal rescue commercials. It is not about spiritual bypassing—spirituality can be a powerful tool, but it is not a shortcut. This is about real emotional power. The kind that does not perform. The kind that regulates

Silence is power.
So is presence.

Your words—or your restraint—either fortify trust or quietly erode it. Whether you speak or stay silent, you are always shaping the emotional climate around you.

Stand as Their Lighthouse

Like it or not, you are someone's emotional lighthouse—often for more people than you realize. Others look to you for stability, for the signal that it is safe to breathe, for an example of how to move through the storm without capsizing. That responsibility may feel invisible, but it is real.

And when the light goes out, those relying on it can lose their bearings.

Do not underestimate that impact. Do not dismiss the steadiness you offer. This is not about performing emotional acrobatics—empathy does not require backflips. It is about holding your ground with quiet strength. Listening before reacting. Pausing before speaking. Staying present when things get hard.

Being steady does not mean absorbing everyone else's chaos or sacrificing yourself in the process. Emotional maturity is knowing how to offer stability *without surrendering your own nervous system*. That balance is rare. And powerful.

The Power of Silence and Presence

Go one level below the obvious. Silence is not the absence of sound; it is the presence of self. Most people avoid it. We fill every pause with noise—opinions, explanations, distractions—because quiet brings us face-to-face with what is unresolved.

But silence is where the work begins. It is where the inner monologue lives: the rehearsed arguments, the distorted stories, the old wounds that still ache. In silence, the polished version drops away, and the truth remains.

This is not just poetic language. Across traditions and research, silence has been recognized as a regulator. Mindfulness practices have taught for centuries that stillness is not emptiness—it is fertile ground. Neuroscience confirms that even brief, intentional pauses calm the nervous system, reduce stress hormones, and improve emotional regulation. Some of the most effective leaders—from monastics to CEOs—use silence as discipline and strategy, because quiet reveals what noise conceals. Silence strips away the stage. No lights. No audience. Just you—and what is actually true.

Building Strength with Quiet Practice

Silence is a practice. Sometimes it starts by telling yourself to shut up for a minute. At first, your mind resists. It races. It tightens. It throws a tantrum. Stay anyway.

Over time, the noise settles. You begin to notice the stories you repeat, the biases steering the wheel, the parts of you still auditioning for approval from an audience that is not watching. That is when silence stops feeling empty and starts feeling clarifying.

This is where emotional intelligence becomes real. It is not about fixing others. It is about holding space without judgment. Everyone is carrying something—loss, joy, fear, hope—each processed in wildly different ways. You do not have to agree with someone's coping style to respect that it exists.

If you believe leadership is command and control, this book will challenge you. If you think nice equals emotionally intelligent, you may feel exposed. If you are clinging to behaviors that keep you reactive or defensive, you will likely get uncomfortable. That is not a flaw. Discomfort is a doorway.

Being emotionally intelligent is not about being the smartest or the nicest. It is about being the safest. The clearest. The one who can hold complexity without collapsing. That is a quiet kind of power.

Leadership—in Life, Not Just at Work

This is not just boardroom leadership. It is parenting. Partnering. Mentoring. Being human when the pressure hits and the mask slips. It is how you show up when titles fade and no one is clapping.

Becoming someone people can exhale around means creating a pocket of calm in a world addicted to chaos. That requires protecting your own peace so you can offer it without depletion. You do not need all the answers. You need presence, honesty, and steadiness.

Trust does not come from résumés or trophies. It grows from values, consistency, and emotional reliability. That is what makes people lean in.

The Work We are Building

Not a collection of ideas. A structure.

There is nothing here to perform and no persona to adopt. The work is grounded, practical, and designed to strengthen emotional clarity, internal regulation, and relational steadiness across real life—at work, at home, and everywhere pressure shows up.

Each section develops a core capacity: how we listen, think, regulate emotion, communicate, and protect energy. Individually, these skills are useful. Together, they form an internal framework that supports clear decision-making, emotional resilience, and trustworthy presence under stress.

The focus is refinement, not accumulation. Rather than adding more strategies or noise, the work builds internal steadiness—the kind that allows a person to remain present, self-aware, and emotionally grounded when circumstances are uncertain or demanding.

What follows are the practices that make that steadiness possible.

Be the First Love of Your Life

Radical self-loyalty is the foundation. This is not narcissism—it is emotional independence. When you stop outsourcing your worth, you become grounded, resilient, and free. Learn how to be the sanctuary you keep seeking elsewhere.

Listening like You Actually Care

Real listening is not waiting to speak. It is shutting down the internal commentary, allowing silence, and staying present long enough to truly understand. This is where connection begins.

The Power of Thought (You Are Not Just a Passenger)

Your brain is not a bystander—it is a pattern machine. Neuroplasticity allows you to interrupt old narratives and choose better ones. You can change the channel.

The Lies We Tell Ourselves

Distortions, avoidance, and negative self-talk quietly shape behavior. This work helps you loosen your grip on those stories so clarity can return.

Know What You Value (or You Will Fall for Anything)

Values are your internal compass. When your life aligns with them, burnout loses its grip and integrity becomes automatic.

Understand Your Worth (It Is Not up for Debate)

Confidence is not volume. It is quiet ownership—neither overperforming nor disappearing.

How Do You Show Up? (Seriously, Take a Look)

Your presence communicates before you speak. Facial expressions, posture, and energy shape how others experience you—often more than your words.

Words Matter, "Dammit!!"

Language can wound or heal in subtle ways. Learn how words shape trust, safety, and connection—often without you realizing it.

Emotional Control Is a Superpower

Calm is not weakness. It is regulation. Responding instead of reacting is one of the clearest markers of emotional mastery.

Trust Is a Verb

Trust is built through action—showing up, speaking up, and following through. Reliability creates safety.

Hidden Genius

Not all leadership is loud. Some of the most effective influence is quiet, steady, and unseen.

Soul Suckers, Energy Vampires, & Emotional Leeches

Learn how to recognize draining dynamics and protect your peace without guilt.

Habits, Tools, and Sanity Saving Practices

Practical tools to support daily regulation, clarity, and resilience.

For Those Ready to Rise

This is not a feel-good self-help book. It is a self-empowerment manual. You are not here to be perfect. You are here to be real.

Each chapter builds a different muscle. Together, they form what I call soul skills—the emotional, mental, and nervous-system strength required to navigate complexity with grace and grit.

Are you ready to love yourself without negotiation? To listen like it matters? To think with intention and trust with clarity?

Then take a breath. Let go of who you think you should be. Step into who you already are.

This is not about soft skills.
This is about soul skills.
This is nervous system–level strength.

This is power.

Welcome to the work.

Part I: It Starts with You — The Inner Work, Self, Mindset, & Emotional Grounding

Everything begins with the relationship you have with yourself. Before presence, communication, or leadership... comes you. Not the version you manage daily, not the one you present to the world—the one who sits quietly inside when the noise fades.

Every interaction you have with the world is filtered through the state of your inner world. When that inner world is tired, overwhelmed, or uncertain, it shows—no matter how composed you appear. You can steady your voice and smooth your expression, but your energy still tells the truth. People may not always know what's off, but they can feel when something is unsettled beneath the surface.

Self-mastery begins with radical self-honesty—the willingness to tell yourself the truth even when it is inconvenient, uncomfortable, or humbling. It means noticing when you minimize your feelings, when you push past your limits, when you say "I'm fine" while your inner world is quietly asking for care. It is learning to stop negotiating against your own needs and start honoring your inner signals as meaningful information rather than interruptions.

From there comes awareness of your thoughts, beliefs, and intentions—because mindset shapes experience. Old stories replay themselves if left unchecked. Outgrown beliefs whisper from the background. When you meet those patterns with curiosity instead of judgment, you begin to choose your responses rather than defaulting to reflex.

Self-mastery is not about perfection; it is about clarity.
Clarity about what grounds you.
Discernment about what matters most.
Commitment to the values you will no longer negotiate away.

The goal is not to become unshakable. The goal is to become
self-loyal.

When you are loyal to yourself, you stop abandoning your needs for
approval and stop shrinking to make others comfortable. You begin
to show up steadier and clearer—rooted in who you are. That is the
kind of presence people trust, even in uncertainty.

This is where the work begins:
Where you stop outsourcing your worth.
Where you stop performing strength you do not actually feel.
Where you start building an inner stability that does not disappear
when someone is disappointed, unimpressed, or uncomfortable.

Because before you can truly listen to others, you have to learn
how to listen to yourself.

Chapter 1:
Be the First Love of Your Life

Radical Self-Loyalty, Emotional Independence, and Sacred Self-Regard

You speak to yourself more than you speak to anyone else on this planet. All day long, in big moments and tiny ones, you narrate your life to yourself. That inner voice layers meaning, judgment, hope, and fear into everything you do (Jung, 1973).

Yet most of us would fire our inner critic if it were a real person. Imagine a coworker following you around all day whispering: *You should have done better... Everyone is going to notice that mistake... Why are you even trying?* You would duck for cover, update your résumé, and block them on every platform you could find.

But when the same words come from within, we believe them. We let that voice dictate our worth, our effort, our right to take up space. We absorb it, nod along, and keep going—as if relentless self-criticism were normal, or worse, necessary.

So here is your first directive: **speak kindly to yourself**. Become the voice that steadies rather than shames. Pause before judgment. Still yourself before criticism.

Because before you can lead others, influence a team, or change the world, you must tend to the one relationship that shapes everything else—your relationship with yourself. Make your own heart and mind the safest place you know. Be the epic love you thought you had to find.

Check Your Compass

When was the last time you truly listened to the tone of your inner voice? Would you speak that way to someone you respect? Your self-talk sets direction—make sure your compass points toward compassion, not criticism.

Radical Self-Loyalty: Not a Scented Candle

Radical self-loyalty is not a feel-good self-care trend you pick up like a scented candle. It is a survival strategy—a bedrock necessity in a chaotic world. It is the commitment to stand so firmly in your truth that external noise no longer pulls you off-center. It is living in alignment with who you are so you stop loaning out your worth, your peace, or your power to other people's approval (Cain, 2012).

We all know the reflex: saying yes because it is easier than explaining. Because you want to be helpful. Because you have always been the reliable one. Radical self-loyalty is the quiet inner voice that says *No*.

Sometimes it looks like declining the meeting that drains more than it delivers. Other times, it is stepping away from a toxic family conversation—even if everyone else is still marinating in the drama. And sometimes, it is simply choosing not to go where your soul is whispering, *"You do not belong here."*

It also lives in the small, unglamorous choices: delaying a non-urgent response, skipping the optional committee, protecting your evenings. These moments add up. They shape a life lived with clarity, integrity, and energy you actually own.

Some will call it selfish. Let them. Choosing yourself is not selfish—it is alignment. It is refusing to gaslight your gut just to keep the peace. It is honoring your boundaries, even when it makes others uncomfortable.

And to be clear: radical self-loyalty does not mean you stop showing up for others. It means you stop abandoning yourself in the process.

Alignment Is a Vote

Every yes is a vote for the life you are building.
Pause before committing and ask whether this choice aligns with your values or drains them. Choose with intention, not obligation.

When Self-Talk Turns Savage

You are the narrator of your life, and the way you speak to yourself matters more than anyone else's opinion (Carlson, 1997). Think about the last time you made a mistake or felt exposed. Did your inner dialogue sound like a wise mentor or a harsh critic eager to keep score?

Most of us default to cruelty without realizing it. *I'm so stupid. How could I mess that up? No wonder no one takes me seriously. Why do I always do this?* These thoughts arrive fast and sharp, often disguised as "motivation" or "accountability." But they are neither. They are shame wearing a productivity mask.

Your inner dialogue is the real battlefield. Radical self-loyalty is tested in the trenches of your own mind, where the inner drill sergeant has unlimited access to a megaphone and zero concern for your well-being. No HR department. No performance review. Just constant commentary.

Think of the last mistake you replayed on loop like it was a Netflix series you couldn't turn off. The typo in that email. The awkward joke that landed wrong. The presentation where your brain evacuated mid-sentence. Did you scold yourself for hours? Days? Weeks?

That is not growth. That is self-abandonment—betraying yourself by letting shame become the soundtrack of your inner world. It keeps you small, hypervigilant, and perpetually braced for rejection that may never come. What if instead of *"I blew it"*, you said, *"That was rough—and I'm still learning. This is a chapter, not the whole book."* What if the mistake became information instead of a verdict?

That shift may sound small, but it is profound. It is your nervous system stepping out of threat mode. It is your brain quietly upgrading its operating system—moving from self-attack to self-correction, from collapse to resilience (Kolb, 1984).

This is what it means to become the nurturing, steady voice you may never have had. Not indulgent. Not dismissive. Honest without being cruel. Supportive without lowering standards.
The next time your mind starts weaponizing shame—replaying mistakes, exaggerating flaws, dragging old regrets into the present—pause and ask yourself:

Would I say this to someone I love?
Would I speak this way to my best friend?
Would I ever want these words spoken to my child?

If the answer is no, they do not deserve residence in your inner dialogue either.

Radical self-loyalty begins here—with the decision to stop being your own worst critic and start becoming your safest place to land.

Choose Your Voice

When your thoughts turn harsh, pause and listen.
Who is leading your inner dialogue—your critic or your ally?
The voice you practice internally becomes the tone you
carry into the world.

Emotional Independence

Radical self-loyalty, emotional independence, and genuine self-regard are inseparable. Self-loyalty gives you the courage to honor your boundaries. Emotional independence allows you to remain steady without needing others to validate you. Self-regard ensures you meet yourself with compassion rather than criticism (Kishimi & Koga, 2013). Together, they form the foundation for showing up fully—in your relationships, your work, and your life.

Emotional independence is often misunderstood. It is not coldness, aloofness, or emotional distance. It is not narcissism dressed up as confidence. It is the opposite of codependency. Emotional independence means you can experience your feelings without outsourcing their regulation. You can soothe your nervous system, name what you feel, and move through discomfort without demanding someone else fix it for you (Laney, 2002).

When you are emotionally independent, you do not cling to relationships out of fear of being alone. You do not crumble when someone disapproves of you or rush to overexplain in hopes of being understood. You can celebrate your wins without waiting for applause and absorb feedback without it becoming a referendum on your worth.

Here is the paradox most people miss: emotional independence does not make relationships colder—it makes them richer. When you stop asking others to carry your emotional weight, you show up as a whole person instead of a half-person searching for completion (Chapman & Campbell, 1997). You listen without defensiveness. You love without desperation. You give without depletion.

Growth, at its core, is an inside job. Developing a personal roadmap—learning how you regulate, recover, and realign—is work only you can do (Kolb, 1984). No one else can walk that terrain for you. And once you do, something shifts; relationships become a place of mutual exchange rather than emotional survival.

Emotional independence does not mean you stop needing others. It means you stop *needing them to be who you become.* You learn how to stand firmly in yourself while still reaching outward with empathy and care.

Love from wholeness, not hunger.
That is the work.

Finding Balance and Seeing the Forest Through the Trees

Picture two trees growing side by side. Their roots are deep, and they lean gently toward each other, offering support—but they do not merge. Each tree has space to grow, to reach toward the sun in its own way, yet their closeness provides strength and resilience. That is emotional interdependence: a healthy dance of connection without loss of self (Greene, 2016).

Codependency is when one tree strangles the other, twisting its growth to meet someone else's needs at the expense of its own. Narcissism is when a tree refuses to lean at all, isolating itself from the forest, cutting off the nourishment and perspective that come from fellowship. And somewhere in the middle, most of us wobble, learning how much to lean, how much to stand, and how to honor both self and others.

Being emotionally independent does not mean you refuse to love or become vulnerable. Quite the opposite, actually. It means you hold your center, respond with empathy, and refuse to be devoured by others' chaos. You check in with your own truth before scanning the room for approval. You remind yourself that you are enough—no matter who is watching. That is radical self-love in practice.

Sacred Self-Regard

Sacred self-regard has been diluted by highlight reels, affirmations, and marketing slogans until it feels hollow. In reality, self-devotion is neither polished nor convenient. It is honest. It is disruptive.

It is a practice you return to again and again—especially on the days when it would be easier to abandon yourself.

Real self-love is not aesthetic. It is gritty. It is choosing truth over comfort and integrity over approval. It is forgiving yourself for mistakes without minimizing them. It is releasing relationships and patterns that feel familiar but keep you small. It protects your peace even when you fear disappointing someone else.

Sacred self-regard shows up in ordinary moments no one applauds. It is resting without guilt because your body is asking for it. It is cancelling plans to protect your mental health, even when it creates tension. It is addressing the boundary that has been crossed instead of swallowing resentment. It is turning off your phone long enough for your nervous system to remember what quiet feels like.

Imagine a day where self-respect is your default setting. You listen to your body instead of overriding it. You tell the truth instead of smoothing it over. You follow through on the thing you have been avoiding—not because it is comfortable, but because honoring yourself matters.

These are not grand gestures. They are everyday acts of self-respect—the quiet revolutions of someone who has decided they matter.

Sacred self-regard grows in these moments. Small. Repeatable. Personal. You guard your energy like it is precious—because it is. You stop waiting for permission to take up space in your own life.

This is radical self-love in practice. Not performative. Not perfect. Devoted. A rhythm you build over time, not a finish line you cross.

Small Sacred Choices

Which quiet act of self-respect is asking to be honored today?
Growth rarely announces itself; it unfolds through small,
consistent choices. Honor one.

Grieving the Loss of Your Past Self

Growth will hurt. Before self-love feels liberating, it often feels lonely. There is grief in becoming—grief for the versions of yourself you have outgrown, the roles you played to survive, the ways you learned to bend so others would stay.

You may feel anger for what you tolerated. Sadness for how long you stayed quiet. Confusion as familiar relationships begin to feel unfamiliar. None of this means you are doing something wrong. It means you are waking up.

Pause here. Take a breath. Let your body catch up to the truth your mind is learning.

Grief is not only about losing people; it is also about releasing identities. The agreeable one. The fixer. The peacemaker. The version of you who believed love required endurance. Letting those selves go can feel like betrayal—even when releasing them is an act of care.

You may ache as you step back from relationships that no longer fit. That ache does not make you disloyal. It makes you honest.

Shared DNA does not entitle someone to mistreat you. Shared history does not require you to stay stuck in it. Letting go does not mean you did not care. It means you finally started caring about yourself, too.

Loneliness can sting when you realize you were the one holding the relationship together. When the emotional labor was not mutual. When survival masqueraded as connection. Seeing that clearly is heartbreaking—but clarity is not cruelty.

Outgrowing people—even family—is not betrayal. It is self-respect. It is the quiet decision to stop confusing familiarity with safety and endurance with devotion.

Grief, in this way, becomes a threshold. You mourn what was, honor what carried you this far, and step forward with more honesty than before. Growth does not move in straight lines—it circles, revisits, and asks for patience.

And when the weight feels heavy, remember this: grief is not pulling you backward. It is making space for who you are becoming.

The Legacy of Feeling Unseen

For many people, the grief runs deeper than what was lost. It reaches back to what was never fully received.

When your voice holds little value early in life, you stop trusting that it matters. You learn to shrink. To adapt. To read the room before you ever read yourself. You become fluent in the emotional language of everyone else while quietly losing your own.

A child who grows up feeling unseen often learns to perform for visibility. They become the helper, the fixer, the one who holds everything together while quietly unraveling. They trade authenticity for approval and call it love. This is not people-pleasing—it is people-proving. Proving you are enough. Proving you are safe to love. Proving your worth through usefulness, excellence, and endurance.

The cost is steep. Profound loneliness. A fatigue that rest does not touch. An identity built around what you provide rather than who you are. You become essential everywhere but at home within yourself.

You learn to anticipate others' emotions before honoring your own. You apologize for needs no one asked you to suppress. You long to be chosen yet hesitate to choose yourself. You want to be supported yet deny yourself rest. You want to be heard yet whisper your truth like it is negotiable.

And here is the turning point: No one is coming to hand you what you did not receive. But this is not despair—it is freedom. Because the moment you realize the healing is yours to claim, no one can withhold it from you.

Being unseen may be part of your origin story, but it does not have to be your ending. You are allowed to stop performing. To take up space. To speak without shrinking. To exist without justification.

When you finally see yourself, the world does not get to pretend you are invisible anymore.

Everyone Has a Story

Everyone has a story. That is the human curriculum. None of us make it through life untouched—we carry invisible chapters shaped by loss, heartbreak, fear, and quiet acts of survival. The question is not whether you have a story. It is how you live it, how you tell it, and whether you let it define you.

At some point, you have to face the stories you carry. The looping narratives shaped by pain—*I am too much. I am not enough. I will never be safe. This is just how it is*—are not truths. They are wounds dressed up as warnings. And the longer they go unexamined, the more authority they gain over your choices.

Awareness is the turning point. When you can name the story, you loosen its grip. You begin to see where fear has been steering, where old survival strategies are still running the show long after the threat has passed. This is not about erasing the past. It is about understanding it well enough to stop repeating it.

If trauma can be passed down through generations, so can healing. So can clarity. So can the courage to choose differently. Every boundary you set, every cycle you end, every moment you choose honesty over chaos—this is legacy work. Quiet, often unseen, but powerful.

Trauma and grief are not flaws. They are part of what life has come to teach you. They are not evidence that you are broken; they are evidence that you endured. What you survived shaped you—but it does not get to own you.

You are not the story that hurt you. You are the one who gets to revise it.

Growth does not move in a straight line. It spirals. It revisits familiar territory with new awareness. It can feel disorienting before it feels peaceful. Imagine the Unalome—the Buddhist symbol of enlightenment—winding, tangled, uncertain, until it slowly straightens. That is how real growth unfolds.

You do not have to stay stuck in the first draft of your life. You are allowed to edit, reinterpret, and reclaim meaning. As an old narrative resurfaces, pause and ask: *How would my wiser self tell this story now? What did this teach me? What no longer belongs in the next chapter?*

This is self-love in practice. Not denial. Not bypassing. The steady, courageous act of owning your story without letting it imprison you.

And when you do, something shifts. What once felt like a wound becomes wisdom. What once held you back becomes a reference point—not a rule.

You carry the story. You are not trapped inside it.

Acceptance, Boundaries, and Becoming the Blueprint

There is no healing without acceptance. You cannot change what you refuse to acknowledge, and you cannot love what you continue to reject. Acceptance is not agreement, approval, or forgiveness on demand. It is truth-telling. And once something is named honestly, it loses its power to control you from the shadows.

Acceptance means allowing the full picture to exist: your strength and your scars, your wisdom and your wounds, the ways you have grown and the ways you are still learning. It means dropping the exhausting effort of pretending you are unaffected or "over it." What you accept, you can work with. What you deny, you remain ruled by.

When you accept yourself this fully, something fundamental shifts. Shame loses leverage. Nobody can weaponize what you already own.

This is where real confidence is born—not from perfection, but from self-possession.

Acceptance naturally gives rise to boundaries. Once you know who you are and what you value, you stop negotiating your worth. You stop explaining yourself to people who benefit from misunderstanding you. You become less interested in being agreeable and more committed to being aligned.

Boundaries are not walls; they are filters. They clarify what is welcome and what is not. They protect your energy, your time, and your emotional health—not because you are rigid but because you are responsible for what you allow into your life. A boundary is simply the external expression of internal clarity.

As boundaries strengthen, so does your presence. You stop shrinking. You stop contorting yourself to fit into rooms that cannot hold you. You become consistent—not reactive, not defensive, not performative. That consistency is what others feel. It is what creates trust.

This is where you begin to become the blueprint.

Not because you announce it. Not because you demand it. But because people notice the way you move through the world. The way you stay grounded under pressure. The way you tell the truth without cruelty. The way you protect your peace without disappearing.

Some will be drawn to this. Others will be unsettled by it. That is not a problem to solve. You are not here to be palatable. You are here to be real.

When you stop abandoning yourself, you give others permission to stop abandoning themselves, too. You show what self-respect looks like in practice—not as a performance, but as a way of being.

Becoming the blueprint does not mean being flawless. It means being anchored. It means modeling what it looks like to live with integrity, to honor boundaries, and to choose self-loyalty even when it would be easier not to.

Start small if you need to: One honest no. One protected boundary. One moment where you choose alignment over approval.

That is how standards are set.
That is how culture shifts.
That is how you lead—without ever needing to say a word.

What You're Willing to Release

What are you still holding on to that your future self has already outgrown? Release is not loss—it is alignment. Integrity is revealed by what you are willing to let go.

The Hidden Cost of Not Choosing Yourself

The cost of not choosing yourself is rarely obvious at first. It shows up quietly—accruing over time—until the balance is suddenly unsustainable.

When you trade your worth for approval, you accept payment in emotional currency that expires quickly. Performance-based love is not love; it is a transaction. And every time you overextend to earn belonging, you withdraw from yourself.

In personal relationships, this often looks like shrinking to be needed. You sacrifice your needs so completely that your identity becomes whoever the other person requires you to be. You mistake loyalty for endurance and tolerance for love. You stay because leaving feels like failure—even when staying costs you your peace.

In professional settings, the pattern wears a different uniform but does the same damage. You say yes while drowning. You become indispensable by over-functioning, praised as reliable while quietly carrying the weight of multiple roles. Responsibility becomes self-sacrifice. Dedication becomes depletion. You disappear behind the work you keep saving.

The most painful cost is internal. When you consistently choose others over yourself, you teach your nervous system that your needs are negotiable. Over time, resentment replaces connection, exhaustion replaces clarity, and self-trust erodes. You begin to feel invisible in your own life.

The tragedy is not that others fail to choose you. It is that you stop choosing yourself first.

Belonging does not require contortion. It does not ask you to betray your values or abandon your boundaries. Real connection begins when you allow yourself to be seen—not for how useful you are but for who you are.

Until you claim that truth, you will keep writing emotional checks your soul cannot afford to cash.

Choosing yourself is not an act of defiance. It is an act of responsibility. It is refusing to shrink for rooms that cannot hold your fullness. It is setting a standard so clear that anything misaligned falls away on its own.

Energy Has a Ledger

Where have you been overdrafting your energy in the name of loyalty or love? Generosity without boundaries becomes depletion. Protect your reserves.

Soulful & Empowering Alternatives: A Love Story with Yourself

You have been searching for sanctuary in other people, hoping someone might finally hold you the way you have always longed to be held. The quiet truth is this: You are the sanctuary.

Be the calm in your own chaos. Make your heart the safe house you return to, not the place you abandon. Treat it as sacred ground—not a doormat.

Fall in love with yourself—and not the polished, performative version. The real one. The devoted, unconditional kind of love you thought someone else was supposed to give you. The kind that heals because it stays.

You do not need to chase love when you become it. Carry your heart like something rare. Guard it. Nurture it. Celebrate it. Do not hand it to people who have not earned the right to hold it.

Stop waiting to be chosen. Choose yourself—like a vow. Tend to your soul as a lifelong relationship, because it is. Be both gardener and garden.

Make your life a story you never get tired of telling. One where you rise, fall, rise again—and grow more devoted to who you are becoming each time.

Above all, choose yourself. Every day.
Because your life depends on it.

Your Inner Sanctuary

If your heart were a sanctuary, what would need to be released— or welcomed—to restore peace? What you allow into your inner space shapes your daily rhythm. Choose with care.

From Self-Love to Presence

What the world needs is not ideal people, but honest, emotionally intelligent ones. It starts with you—the one who is there when you wake up, when things fall apart, when you celebrate, and when you survive heartbreak. You are your longest commitment. It is time to treat yourself that way.

So go be the love of your own damn life.

When you do—when you begin meeting yourself with the same respect and care you have given so freely to others—something shifts. You move differently. You show up differently. Not just for others, but for yourself.

You stop skimming the surface of connection and begin experiencing its depth. You stop hearing words and start listening for meaning.

Because when you finally feel seen by yourself, you stop demanding that validation from every interaction. You create space—for presence, for clarity, for genuine resonance.

And that is when listening changes.
It is no longer a tactic or a checkbox.
It becomes a practice.
A form of respect.
A reflection of who you are.

Because the way you listen tells the truth about you—your values, your sense of worth, your emotional maturity.

So let's talk about that next.
And how being the first love of your life shapes not only how you show up for others but how fully you show up for yourself.

Becoming the Love of Your Life

Coming Home to Yourself

Before moving forward, take a breath and settle into yourself. What does loving yourself look like in practice, not theory? Peace begins when you stop searching for it outside yourself.

The Peace Trade

Where have you been trading your peace to keep someone else comfortable? Compromise is healthy; self-abandonment is not. Protect the calm that clarity creates.

Your Safest Home

Which part of you is ready to be met with compassion instead of criticism? What would it mean to make your own heart your safest place to land? Every act of gentleness opens the door to wholeness.

Chapter 2: Listening like You Actually Care

The Real Skills of Active Listening

Welcome to life with the volume cranked up. We live in a noisy world, sometimes overwhelmingly so. From the moment we wake up to the moment we collapse into bed, relentless streams of voices, alerts, expectations, and distractions compete for our attention. We are over-communicating and under-connecting. We respond to everything and connect to almost nothing.

And in those rare, fragile moments when the world goes quiet... we squirm. We scroll, tap, click, multitask—anything to avoid what stillness might reveal. But here is the truth: Growth lives in the stillness. You cannot hear yourself—your needs, your intuition, your truth—through external noise and the static of everyone else's voices. Silence is a mirror. It is not empty; it is full of answers. And yes, it can be uncomfortable, because silence does not lie. It reveals—if you let it.

The Quiet Truth

When the noise fades, what truth rises that you most want to avoid—and most need to hear? Stillness reveals what distraction hides. Listen gently.

Listening is not a competitive sport. Most people do not actually listen—they wait for their turn to speak, rehearse their rebuttal, or drift mentally while another person is talking. Imagine trying to follow a movie while scrolling through your phone—you miss the nuance, the plot, the emotional core. Distracted listening does the same to relationships (Forni, 2012).

To truly listen is to offer something sacred: your full attention. Attention heals. It validates. It reduces anxiety and builds trust. It supports emotional regulation, strengthens memory, and raises self-worth—for both the speaker and the listener. It says: You matter enough for me to show up fully.

Really listening is a gift you give to another person that matters.

The Gift of Undivided Attention

When was the last time you gave someone your full attention—no phone, no agenda, just presence? In a world addicted to distraction, attention is rare. And it speaks admiration louder than words.

Active listening requires parking your ego at the door. You do not listen to correct, fix, or control. You listen to understand. And you do it with your whole self—mind, body, heart, and yes, your full physical presence. This is not passive. It is active, deliberate, and transformational. It allows you to rid yourself, even momentarily, of the transactional self (Forni, 2012).

Real listening is uncomfortable at times. It asks you to slow down when the world demands speed. It asks you to feel when avoidance seems easier. It asks you to witness the raw, messy humanity in others—and, sometimes, in yourself. But every time you do, you strengthen the muscle that matters most: your brain's ability to meet life as it is, not as you wish it to be (Kolb, 1984).

Silence and attentiveness are not soft skills; they are essential life skills. And the better you get at them, the more you realize that every conversation,every interaction, every pause is an opportunity. Not to win. Not to impress. Not to perform—but to truly show up for yourself and others.

The Listening Mirror

Do you listen to understand—or to defend what you already believe? True listening requires releasing your rebuttal long enough for another truth to exist. Notice what shifts when you do.

Listening Is a Physical Practice

Sit down. Put the phone down. Make eye contact. Mirror their posture if it feels natural. Let your entire body say I am here. Because it is—your body is part of the conversation, whether you realize it or not. It often speaks louder than your words.

Fidgeting, crossed arms, glancing at the clock or the door—these micro-signals can send messages you never meant to deliver. So, listen with your whole body. Let your stillness communicate safety. Let your presence be felt. People know when you are fully with them. They feel it when you lean in with intention—or when you quietly pull away.

Beyond what is being said, listen for the spaces in between—the pauses, the sighs, the tension in their shoulders. The loudest parts of a story are often told in silence. Your physical presence is not passive; it is active, embodied, and deeply human. The quiet between sentences can reveal what words cannot carry.

Watch their eyes—not to interrogate, but to witness. Do they light up? Flicker with discomfort? Drift away when something lands too close to home? Notice when they lean in or check out. A drop in energy, a wandering gaze, a shift in posture may signal a change in trust or emotional availability. Your job is not to diagnose. Your job is to notice.

Listening is less about collecting words and more about sensing the whole person. It is not just what they say but how they say it, what they avoid, and whether your presence makes it safer for them to say more.

We often fall into the trap of believing that more words equal better leadership or clearer communication. That is rarely true. When you overcommunicate but under-connect, you miss the point of human interaction. At work, this shows up as information overload—meeting monologues, endless slides, rapid-fire messages—without checking whether anyone feels heard or able to absorb what is being said.

In personal life, the pattern is similar. You manage logistics but miss the emotional weather. You offer pep talks instead of presence. You speak to people without slowing down enough to be with them.

In both settings, the issue is the same: mistaking speaking for connecting. More words do not build trust. Listening does. Curiosity does. Space does.

And for the love of everything holy—stop repeating yourself at increasing decibel levels. Volume does not equal clarity. It only makes listening harder.

The Body Speaks First

How does your body listen—do you lean in, brace, or drift away?
Your posture often communicates before your words do.
Let your body signal safety.

Silence Shapes Our Deepest Experiences

There are moments in life where words fail entirely. In the most meaningful chapters of another person's life, all that remains is presence—and the discipline to stay.

Those who have stood beside someone at the end of life understand this truth: you cannot fix what is unfixable. You cannot explain it away or soften it with language. You can only witness it. And in those moments, that is everything (Albom, 1997).

Silence in these spaces is not awkward—it is sacred. It makes room for dignity, for grief, for preparation. Sometimes the most powerful act is the willingness to show up, shut up, and stay.

This kind of listening is not passive. It requires steadiness when nothing can be done. It asks you to resist the urge to fill space with reassurance or solutions that do not exist. To hold a hand without clinging. To sit without performing. To remain present when discomfort would prefer distraction.

That presence leaves a mark. Not just on the person being witnessed, but on the one who stays. It teaches a different kind of strength—the ability to stand in truth without turning away, to feel deeply without hardening, to offer compassion without needing control.

This is listening in its most honest form. Not nodding politely. Not waiting for your turn. Choosing to be fully there when words are powerless.

And while few moments carry the gravity of life's final chapters, the skill is transferable. Every day, people bring quiet grief, fear, and vulnerability into conversations. They are not always asking for answers. Often, they are asking—without saying—to be met with steadiness.

Silence, when practiced with intention, becomes a form of respect. A signal that says: *You are not alone. I can stay with this.*

This is the kind of listening that changes people.
And it begins by learning when not to speak.

Stop Preparing Your Comeback While They Are Still Talking

Listening is hard—especially when your own biases, assumptions, and opinions are loud in the background. It asks you to quiet your internal narrator: the part of you scripting a counterargument, judging, analyzing, defending, diagnosing. We all carry filters and stories—about ourselves and about others. Active listening asks you to pause those. To suspend judgment. To recognize that someone else's reality may be very different from yours—and still valid.

You do not always need to speak. You do not always need the last word or the payoff. But you can be a steady light for someone else's darkness. That is maturity. That is emotional courage.

Our energy matters. Even when the words are right, if your presence signals distraction or impatience—I'm bored, I'm waiting, I'm planning my response—people feel it. They may nod along, but internally they begin to retreat, protecting themselves from a listener who is not fully there.

Empathy is the quiet power behind real listening. You do not have to agree to empathize. You do not have to fix anything to hold space. Often, the most healing words are simple: I hear you. Not a solution. Not a lecture. Just presence. Telling someone to calm down has never worked; being genuinely heard often does.

When people feel seen, their bodies respond. Shoulders soften. Defenses lower. They move out of survival mode and into engagement. Most people are not searching for answers—they are searching for acknowledgment. For someone willing to witness their struggle, their hope, their heartbreak.

Listening is not about getting it right every time. It is a skill, yes—but also a mindset. You will interrupt. You will get triggered. You will slip into old habits. Welcome to being human. Awareness is the reset button. Come back. Regroup. Every conversation offers another chance.

No one holds a monopoly on truth. Every lens is imperfect—including yours. Listen for the angle you might be missing. Someone else has lived a life you have not.

Listening, in the end, is a promise: You are safe here. I will not rush you. I will not hijack your story with mine. I will stay. The way you respond when someone is vulnerable matters. It shapes their sense of safety, their sense of worth, and their willingness to be open again.

Sometimes it is the smallest gestures—slowing your speech, softening your tone, leaning in—that make the greatest difference. When you stop rehearsing your rebuttal, you make room for someone else to be fully seen. And in doing so, you become the kind of listener the world needs more of.

Choose Your Tribe with Care

If silence is the truest test of presence, then the company you keep reveals how much of it you can stand. Not everyone deserves front-row seats in your life. Your tribe may be small; you will know them not by what they say but by how they show up when words fall short.

The people who matter most are not always the most obvious. They are not the ones making promises in neon or appearing only when it is convenient. They are the ones whose actions align with care. The ones who notice how you really feel, not just what you manage to package into acceptable words. They sense the sigh behind your smile, the hesitation in your voice, the quiet weight you carry—and they do not look away.

This kind of emotional availability cannot be faked. It is not about saying the right thing at the right time. It is about being able to sit in silence without panicking to fill it. About understanding that listening is not a polite intermission before delivering a monologue but a skill worth practicing. Presence alone can carry a conversation—no pretense, no invisible scoreboard tracking who gives or takes more.

True belonging has less to do with the size of your circle and more to do with its quality. For many, the invite list is intentionally short and deliberately curated. It consists of the ones who already know where the forks live, who let themselves in, who do not need scripts or stage directions to belong. They treat showing up as a practice, not a performance.

Here is the catch: it's rarely about grand gestures or perfectly timed words. Presence is about showing up fully, exactly as you are, and allowing others to do the same. That kind of authenticity is magnetic. It says: You do not have to earn your place here.

Choose your tribe carefully. The people closest to you shape your sense of belonging more than any book, podcast, or keynote ever could. They set the emotional climate you live in. They either reinforce your boundaries or trample them. They either celebrate your growth or quietly resent it. They either meet you with grace or keep score as if connection were a competitive sport.

A healthy circle does not keep ledgers. It does not measure worth in favors returned or effort tallied. It lives in reciprocity: the understanding that care flows both ways—not always equally, but always sincerely.

And it is not enough to find those people. You must be that person. The one who makes space. The one who listens deeply. The one who can sit with discomfort without rushing to fix it. Belonging is built in these small, steady moments—not grand declarations.

There will always be people who cannot sit in silence with you. They will rush to fill it, distract from it, or cover discomfort with easy clichés. They often mean well, but over time, that noise becomes exhausting. Not everyone deserves unlimited access to your energy.

The gift of a true tribe is that you do not have to wear armor. You do not have to translate your sighs into full sentences. They notice. They witness. They stay.

At its core, the tribe you choose is not about quantity but resonance. It is the people whose presence steadies you—even in silence. Hold them close. And when it is your turn, be that steady ground for them, too.

Active Listening Changes Everything

In the end, active listening is not just about hearing words—it is about hearing people. It is a way of being, a refusal to skim the surface. It means showing up with focus, being open to emotional curiosity, and practicing the courage to shut up, sit down, and truly pay attention. People do not need fixing. They need witnessing. And when you listen like you genuinely care, people notice. More importantly, they remember.

But listening is not only about others. It is also about tuning in to yourself. Because the deepest connection you will ever have is with your own mind. And just as listening to another person requires attention and availability, so does listening to your own inner voice.

Here is the truth: You are not simply a passenger in your story. The thoughts you entertain shape the narrative you live. They can limit you or liberate you. They can drag you back into old patterns, or they can open new possibilities.

That is where we go next: the power of thought. How your inner dialogue can become your greatest ally—or your most relentless critic. And how learning to guide it with intention can transform not only your life but the way you show up for everyone around you.

Listen Like It Matters

Let the Silence Work

Think of the last moment you sat in silence with someone.
Did you rush to fill it—or did you trust it?
Quiet often carries meaning words cannot hold.

Step Out of Rehearsal

When do you catch yourself preparing a response instead of
staying present? Notice the impulse—then release it.
Curiosity begins where control ends.

Front Row or Balcony?

Who earns front-row access to your presence—and who needs
more distance? Not everyone deserves the same level of
emotional proximity. Listening well includes choosing wisely.

Chapter 3:
The Power of Thought (You Are Not Just a Passenger)

"The mind is everything. What you think, you become."

— Buddha

Change Your Mind, Change Your Life

Your thoughts are not background noise. They are the architects of your reality. Every choice you make, every word you speak, every relationship you hold is filtered through the lens of your own mind. Change your thoughts and the world itself looks different. Leave them unchecked, and you risk living inside a story you never chose to write.

Mindset is the steering wheel of your life. The way you think directs your focus, shapes your emotions, and drives your behavior. It can either trap you in loops of stress, self-doubt, and overreaction, or it can open space for clarity, courage, and possibility.

This is not about blind positivity. It is about power. The power to recognize that you are not just along for the ride: You set the course. And when you learn to work with your brain rather than against it, you stop outsourcing your peace and start claiming responsibility for your own experience.

The Story You're Living

What story are you living that you never consciously chose?
Every belief left unquestioned becomes a plotline.
Awareness is the first edit.

The Brain You Inherited

The ability to shift your thoughts is universal. It does not hinge on where you live, the titles on your résumé, or your relationship status. Age does not limit it. Upbringing does not cancel it out. You do not need advanced degrees or a personal coach to access your own thoughts.

What often gets overlooked is how much influence those thoughts actually have. We treat a positive mindset like a nice-to-have accessory: *Stay positive. Think happy thoughts.* Helpful reminders, sure—but if you have ever been ambushed by anxiety in the grocery store or stuck replaying imaginary arguments, you know it is not that simple.

You do not need mantras—you need practice. Thoughts are not background décor; they are the operating system of your life. When the system has bugs, everything glitches. When it is updated, things run more smoothly.

Here is what makes this powerful: new thoughts create new neural connections. Each time you notice a negative path, take a breath, and choose even a slightly better thought, you activate a different route in your brain. At first, it feels awkward—like carving a trail through dense forest. But repetition clears the path. Over time, that trail becomes a walkway. Keep going, and it becomes a highway.

This is not belief—it is biology. Your brain is wired for change. Neuroplasticity shows that the brain reorganizes itself through repeated experience. Every intentional shift in thinking builds new structures—scaffolding for a stronger mind.

The real question is whether you are putting that wiring to work. Whether you are twenty-five or seventy, your brain does not discriminate. The capacity to change is there. The choice is yours.

So why does it feel like such a battle? Because you are not starting from neutral. You are running on an ancient operating system—the survival brain. Its job has always been to scan for danger, avoid pain, and react quickly. That vigilance once protected us from physical threats, but now often misfires in response to criticism, uncertainty, or emotional discomfort.

Your brain is also slow to upgrade. The same instincts that once kept us alive now sound alarms over unanswered emails and awkward silences. Social rejection triggers the nervous system the same way physical danger once did. One negative moment outweighs a dozen positive ones—not because you are dramatic, but because your brain prioritizes threat over joy.

The result is predictable: criticism becomes breaking news while joy gets filed away like a skipped ad. One harsh comment can drown out ten genuine compliments. This imbalance is not a personal failing—it is wiring. The good news is that wiring can be retrained.

The Thought on Repeat

Which thought gets priority in your mind—threat or possibility?
That bias isn't weakness; it's wiring. Wiring can be retrained.

Your Peace, Your Power

Here is the truth: you cannot outsource your peace. **Your peace is your responsibility.** Your joy is your responsibility. If you hand the steering wheel of your life to someone else, do not be surprised when you end up somewhere you never intended to go. Waiting for another person to drive you to happiness is not just unrealistic—it is a crash waiting to happen.

Owning your mind is not about being flawless. It is about practice and consistency. Some days you will slip back into old routes. That is normal. What matters is not whether you ever wander into the weeds—it is whether you keep clearing the new path. Over time, your chosen thoughts stop being effortful and start being natural.

The power of thought is not abstract. It is the quiet, daily work of shaping your own mind so that it supports, rather than sabotages, the life you want.

Reality Check Required

Let's talk about expectations: the ones you place on yourself and the ones you place on others.

Start with your own. Are they grounded in who you actually are or in the version you wish you were? Ignoring your strengths and limitations sets you up to stumble. You cannot build a life on delusion, no matter how polished it looks. Shiny floors do not fix shaky foundations. It is like striving to meet society's version of success—titles, status, income—while ignoring the quiet pull of what actually brings you alive.

Unrealistic expectations will quietly undo you. Stumbling is not always about lack of ability—it is often about chasing standards that were never rooted in our truth. Sometimes what feels like failure is just friction from trying to live inside expectations that do not fit.

Now turn the lens outward. What are you expecting from others? Are you holding someone to a standard you never communicated, or expecting a version of them they never agreed to be?

Disappointment often masquerades as truth. Sometimes it is poor communication in a fancy costume. Before you label someone as unreliable or uncaring, ask yourself: Did I ever actually say what I needed, or did I just assume they should know?

People are not mind readers. And even if they were, they would likely tune out before the story even begins.

Expectation Audit

Which expectations—of yourself or others—are unspoken or unrealistic? Disappointment often signals misalignment, not failure. Clarity begins with naming what you never said out loud.

Thoughts Drive Expectations

Expectations do not come from thin air. They are born from the way you think, the beliefs you carry, and the mental scripts you have rehearsed—sometimes since childhood. Your mind is not a runaway train. It is not meant to be hijacked by guilt, regret, or outdated beliefs. You are the conductor, capable of rerouting and reshaping your thoughts with steady practice and intention.

Hope is not a credit card you swipe only in emergencies. It is not something you dig out when life collapses, when you are out of options, or when you're desperate for rescue. Hope is a daily investment in your inner strength—a quiet, steady commitment to shaping your inner world so your outer world does not swallow you whole. It is choosing thoughts that create oxygen instead of suffocation. It is training your mind to look for possibility instead of inevitability, direction instead of doom. Hope isn't denial; it's discipline. It is the practice of reminding your nervous system, your heart, and your mind that growth is still possible, that change is still possible, that you are still possible.

Let go of internalized idealistic expectations, shame, and regrets that weigh you down. Mistakes do not define you; they refine you.

The goal is forward movement, not an ideal execution. These small choices are additional reps for your mental muscles, reinforcing the pathways you have already started building.

The truth is simple: Thoughts shape lives. The way you think shapes the way you live. This is mindset—the not-so-gentle art of choosing your own experience.

The Outgrown Identity

When your mind drifts, where does it go by default? Familiar doesn't mean true. Noticing the loop gives you the remote.

Positive Thinking vs. Emotional Control

Your thoughts are not passive commentary; they are tools shaping your reality. **What you think influences how you feel, how you feel influences what you do, and what you do reinforces the cycle of thought and perception.**

Positive thinking is the conscious practice of directing your mind toward optimism, possibility, and perspective. It is not naive denial or toxic optimism. It is about noticing challenges clearly while refusing to be defined by them. It is the shift from asking, *"Why is this happening to me?"* to wondering, *"What can I learn, adjust, or appreciate in this moment?"*

Emotional control, or regulation, goes deeper. It is the ability to manage your internal state across thoughts, feelings, and behaviors, particularly in stressful or triggering situations. It allows you to notice the emotional triggers, understand the physiological and cognitive responses they provoke, and then respond intentionally rather than reacting impulsively. Where positive thinking sets the lens, emotional control fine-tunes the focus. Together, they form a powerful foundation for resilience, clear judgment, and interpersonal effectiveness.

Think of positive thinking as the gardener planting seeds in fertile soil—your mindset, beliefs, and resonance. Emotional control is the gardener's hands, pruning and shaping growth so those seeds flourish instead of being choked by weeds of rumination or reactivity. Both are necessary; one without the other leaves potential untapped.

Your First Thought Tells on You

What thought deserves your attention right now—and which doesn't? Pause creates choice. Choice creates authorship.

The Lazy Brain Villain: Default Mode Network & The Art of Mental Muting

Not every drain on your mindset comes from the outside. Sometimes the loudest thief of emotional regulation lives right between your ears. It is not always the negative coworker or the toxic friend—it is your own brain on autopilot, running the same tired loops without your permission. That is when you meet the real villain: the Default Mode Network. Think of it as the backseat driver of your thoughts—the static generator you never asked for.

Here is the unflattering truth: your brain is evolutionarily lazy. It prefers the path of least resistance, which means it loops the same thoughts on repeat—often negative, always familiar. The Default Mode Network (DMN) is the system that hums in the background when you are not focused on a task. It fuels the endless inner monologue, the spiraling what ifs, the reruns of old conversations that still wake you up at night. Left unchecked, it masquerades as reflection while quietly feeding rumination and distraction (Raichle et al., 2001).

If you have ever walked away from a meeting replaying what you should have said or spent your commute catastrophizing about problems that have not yet happened, you have felt the DMN take the wheel. It thrives in idle moments and mental downtime. And while it is not inherently bad—it helps with planning, memory, and self-reflection—it becomes a problem when its default setting slips into obsessive loops, self-criticism, or fear-based storytelling.

The goal is not to fight the DMN—it is to manage it. This is where small, intentional interventions matter. Some people use visual anchors—simple notes like *Shhh* or *Come back*—that act as breadcrumbs to the present moment. Others rely on mental cues: pausing, naming the thought (*that's worry... that's rehearsal*), or taking one conscious breath before re-engaging.These small disruptions activate the brain's executive control systems, nudging the DMN out of the driver's seat and bringing attention back online. Even modest practices—brief mindfulness, structured breaks, deliberate shifts in focus—strengthen your capacity to regulate attention and impulse.

Over time, this builds inner steadiness. It becomes easier to interrupt spirals, return to yourself, and choose your thoughts instead of being carried by them.

The key is perspective: the chatter of the DMN is not truth—it is habit. Old wiring. Familiar, but not always accurate. Some thoughts are useful signals; others are just noise. Learning to tell the difference restores choice.

Yes, the brain is lazy—but it is also remarkably trainable. The DMN does not need to be silenced; it can be redirected and even harnessed for insight. This is the art of mental muting: not shutting the mind down but choosing when, where, and how to listen.

The roommate in your head may still be talking—but now you are the one holding the remote.

Mindset in Action: Focus, Pause, and Redirect

How do you begin? Start with what you focus on. Notice the small glimmers around you—the sweetness, the absurdity, the smile exchanged between strangers, the moment someone holds the door, the sunlight on your floor.

These moments are not small. They are anchors. They pull you back from the edge and remind you that goodness still exists, even when your mind is in full DEFCON mode.

Happiness is not the goal—it is the byproduct. It grows when your thoughts, choices, relationships, and values are aligned. It grows when you live with integrity and show up consciously.

Consider this: how do you see the world? As a threat? A burden? A battlefield? Or as a place of possibility, where each moment offers a chance to redirect your mind and rewire your experience?

Because how you see the world shapes what you experience in it. You are not just a passenger in your mind—you are the driver. Your mind is the landscape of your daily life. Choose wisely. Think bravely. The most powerful real estate you will ever own is the space between your ears.

Understanding the concepts is only the beginning. The real work is daily application. Start by noticing the constant chatter in your mind. Not every thought deserves attention. Some are background noise, habitual loops, or distorted interpretations of reality. This is where mental muting matters: pause, name the thought, and decide whether to engage or let it pass.

Buy yourself a breath before you spend your words. When irritation, anxiety, or defensiveness rises, observe the thought without judgment and ask: Is this true? Helpful? Necessary? Often, it is none of the above. Catch distortions like catastrophizing or all-or-nothing thinking and reframe them with intention. These small mental reps strengthen pathways for calm, clarity, and constructive action.

Redirect your attention toward what you can influence: moments of beauty, intentional connection, and possibility. Focus less on what you cannot control and more on what grounds you. Over time, this builds a mental environment where optimism is practiced, challenges are manageable, and emotional responses are measured rather than automatic.

This is not about denying reality. Life is hard, and pain is unavoidable. But you can choose which narratives you feed and which loops define your day. Thoughts shape perception; perception shapes experience. By learning to notice, pause, and redirect, you reclaim agency over your inner world—and how you meet the outer one.

Quiet the Noise, Choose the Lens

Practice quieting your inner commentary. Not every mental rabbit hole deserves exploration. Tell your inner monologue to take a seat. Disengage from spirals that go nowhere and redirect your focus toward constructive possibilities and grounded what-ifs.

What hijacks your peace also hijacks your relationships. We enter conversations not to connect, but to be heard, validated, or proven right. While our minds rehearse lines, the real substance—the meaning, the emotion, the opportunity for understanding—slips past unnoticed. The thoughts you dwell on don't just shape your inner world; they shape how you meet other people.

When attention is fragmented, perception narrows. You miss subtle cues—the pause before a response, the shift in posture, the sigh that carries more than fatigue. Communication is not just words; it is energy, tone, and presence. The person who is attentive always understands more than the one who is busy.

The power of thought is not about control; it is about clarity. This takes practice, especially in emotional territory where most of us were never taught how to slow down or stay with ourselves. It is a discipline, not a performance.

Mindset is what you choose to amplify. You can acknowledge pain without surrendering to it. You can have a hard day and still believe in better ones. This is emotional intelligence in practice—holding reality and possibility at the same time.

Mental Energy Management

You are shaped by what you repeatedly think. Just as your physical diet affects your body, your mental diet affects your experience of life. Feed your mind resentment, guilt, or fear and that is the environment you live in. Go looking for conflict or confirmation of the worst, and you will find it—your brain is very efficient at that.

Treat your mental space with intention. Clear out beliefs that no longer serve you. Reduce clutter so your thoughts can move and settle. Think of it as mental architecture—arranging your inner world so energy flows, distractions recede, and focus has room to breathe.

A growth mindset is not about forcing optimism; it is about staying available to change. Shift your lens and you begin to see yourself— and others—as you are and as you're becoming, not through the distortion of old stories or assumptions.

For sensory-sensitive people and introverts, overstimulation is not a flaw—it's information. Constant noise, chatter, and background demand drain energy quickly. Silence and stillness are not luxuries; they are necessities for clarity and regulation. Sometimes the most productive thing you can do is absolutely nothing.

Finally, stop narrating yourself into panic or smallness. No one is watching you as closely as you think—they are busy starring in their own internal dramas. Take a breath. Reclaim authorship. If that inner critic insists on sticking around, give it a better job—one that supports you instead of undermining you.

Because in the end, the power of thought is the power of authorship. You are not just a passenger. Every thought you choose is a line in the story you are writing. Write it with intention.

The Lies We Tell Ourselves

Once you realize you can choose your thoughts, the real work begins—seeing the ones you have avoided, noticing the stories you accepted without question, and confronting the beliefs that have been running on autopilot for years.

Welcome to *The Lies We Tell Ourselves.*

This is where we stop letting old narratives run the show. This is where we shine a light on the quiet, shadowed thoughts that whisper, *"I am not enough... They will leave if they really know me... I must do everything perfectly or I have failed."*

These distortions are not truth. They are fear dressed as logic—mental habits that quietly undermine your peace, your clarity, and your relationship with yourself and others.

Get ready to spot them, challenge them, and start telling yourself the truth instead. Because if mindset is the steering wheel, this is the map—the part of the journey where you finally see the roads you have been driving on autopilot and decide which are worth traveling. Peace begins when you stop rereading the old chapter and start writing the next one.

Write Your Own Script

Rewrite the Loop

What belief keeps looping—and what truth could replace it?
Repetition builds reality. Choose the thought
you want reinforced.

Author the Next Line

If you are writing your inner narrative, what comes next?
Let it move you toward calm, not control.
The next thought shapes the next chapter.

Clearing the Mental Room

If your thoughts were a room, would it feel crowded or clear?
Name one belief you're ready to release.
Space is where peace enters.

Chapter 4:
The Lies We Tell Ourselves

The Comfort of the Cage

As we have discovered, the Default Mode Network—the brain's narrator—never stops its chatter when left unrestrained. It fills silence with commentary, predictions, and stories from the past, often with remarkable confidence. Sometimes the voice sounds gentle, wrapped in caution or care: *Do not try that—you might fail. Stay quiet—it feels safer.*

This inner commentary whispers just enough truth to feel credible but twists it into a story that keeps you small. That voice is influenced by evolutionary wiring that overweighs risk and threat, making small concerns feel disproportionately urgent (Baumeister et al., 2001).

The problem is that the DMN does not deliver facts—it tells stories. The content is often loosely based on something real, but the proportions are wildly distorted. A small risk becomes catastrophic. A passing doubt hardens into a defining truth. A single stumble becomes "proof" of permanent inadequacy. The DMN knows exactly which levers to pull. It has been observing you for years, collecting fears, insecurities, and vulnerable moments, and it is not shy about weaponizing them the instant you consider stepping outside familiar lines (Raichle et al., 2001).

Sometimes the DMN truly wants to protect you. That inner voice is not always the villain—it often begins as a guardian, a cautious part of you that remembers the sting of disappointment, the ache of rejection, and emotional echoes you may not consciously recall. It wants to spare you from those wounds. But when that instinct to protect calcifies into avoidance, comfort becomes something else entirely. Comfort weaponized by fear becomes a cage—soft, cushioned, and deceptively safe, yet lined with invisible bars that quietly restrict growth. You tell yourself you are "fine" because discomfort is absent, but what is missing is vitality, movement, and expansion.

Ignored, pain does not vanish; it festers. It sinks below the surface, disguising itself as restlessness, irritation, or that quiet unease that lingers even when everything appears fine. Unattended pain becomes anxiety that refuses logic, a constant distraction, or the inability to truly exhale, even in places meant to feel safe.

Trauma does not disappear—it adapts. It hides in the corners of our awareness, shaping the stories we tell ourselves about who we are and what we deserve. It becomes the invisible hand guiding our reactions, our tone, our distance. It insists on being acknowledged—not to punish but to free us.

The moment we face it, even briefly, something shifts. We reclaim authority over our inner world. We interrupt the autopilot narrative that has been running the show for years. It is rarely dramatic; more often it is a quiet recognition, a steadying pause, a flicker of awareness that says, *"Wait. I see you."*

From that moment on, we are no longer captives of the old story. We begin the slow, deliberate work of rewriting it—line by line, belief by belief—until what once confined us becomes something we can witness without being consumed by.

The Voice That Guides You

When was the last time your inner voice protected your peace—and when did it keep you small? Notice the tone it uses today. The story you believe becomes the life you live.

Rewriting the Script

Left unchecked, the brain's default narrator seizes the wheel, turning fleeting doubts into rigid narratives and small fears into lifelong limitations. Life becomes an act dictated by inherited stories and unconscious beliefs—scripts we did not write—shaped through years of avoidance and self-protection (Jung, 1973).

Awareness interrupts this cycle. Recognizing its voice, noticing distortions, and facing the feelings we have been running from creates space to reclaim authorship. Once we see the inner narrator for what it is—a survival mechanism, not truth—it loses authority. That moment of recognition is liberation: the chance to question, challenge, and rewrite the stories that no longer serve us.

The next step is deliberate: naming the lies, observing their patterns, and loosening their grip. This is not about silencing the voice completely—its caution may still serve—but about deciding which stories deserve your attention and which are ready to be reframed or released. From here, you shift from survival to intentional living, from passive repetition to conscious creation.

The stories that hold us back often sound logical, even kind—until we see how much they cost us. Awareness exposes the quiet bargains we have made with fear and comfort. The work begins not in judgment, but in recognition.

The Author's Seat

What story have you been living that no longer fits who you are becoming? Notice the words you use with yourself—are they protection or permission? Rewriting begins the moment you choose authorship over autopilot.

The Hidden Face of Avoidance

If the lies we tell ourselves are the script, thought avoidance is the stage where the play keeps running. It is the quiet agreement we make with our inner narrator: *Don't look too closely, and maybe it will hurt less.*

Avoidance seems harmless at first. That voice promises relief: *Do not open that box. Do not ask that question. Do not sit in the silence—it will only make things worse.* But avoidance does not protect us; it weakens us. Resilience is built through exposure, not through sidestepping discomfort. Strength comes from meeting challenges, sitting with them, and proving to yourself that they can be endured and overcome. Avoidance may feel like armor, yet it quietly drains your strength, leaving you emotionally fragile, mentally unsettled, and spiritually untested.

Thought avoidance is far more sophisticated than simple procrastination. It wears disguises: busyness, productivity, even success. We overcommit and overschedule—not because we truly want more, but because slowing down feels dangerous. Truth speaks in the quiet, and we are not always ready to hear it. We insist, "All good here!" while hiding beneath layers of activity. The mind races forward, but the soul suffocates from neglect.

Stillness can feel terrifying when the inner world is unsettled. In silence, the inner narrator turns up the volume: buried grief surfaces, unprocessed anger rises, and fears we thought we outran catch up to us. What we avoid does not dissolve; it accumulates. Avoidance is like stacking unopened letters on the counter. Ignore them for weeks, months, even years—eventually, the pile becomes impossible to step around.

And this is where grounded presence begins—not by running from the whispers, but by daring to face them (Kozak, 2019).

The Unopened Letters

*What truth have you been sidestepping or avoiding under
the disguise of busyness or self-protection? Name it—without
judgment, without rushing to fix it. Even unopened, truth waits
patiently to be acknowledged.*

Thought Avoidance & Thought Distortions: From Avoidance to Clarity

Unclenching the mind begins with recognizing a simple truth: **Not all feelings are facts.** Intense reactions often stem from old wounds, unconscious beliefs, or familiar narratives that feel true without actually being accurate. Anxiety and distress usually arise not from the present moment itself but the stories we wrap around it—interpretations, assumptions, and imagined outcomes (Greene, 2016).

Many strong emotions respond to threats that exist primarily in our heads. Clarity begins when we notice those narratives and question them instead of obeying them.

This is where cognitive distortions take root—subtle patterns that twist perception just enough to feel real. They explain, assign blame, and protect pride, but at a cost. They narrow perspective, reinforce limitation, and quietly shape how we experience ourselves and the world (Baumeister et al., 2001). Awareness—pausing, observing, questioning—loosens their grip.

Resisting change is often just resisting uncertainty. Letting go of outdated narratives can feel threatening because it unsettles the ego and disrupts what is familiar. Reactivity may feel protective, but it rarely leads to growth. Thoughtfulness asks more: listening beneath rehearsed defenses, tolerating ambiguity, and choosing presence over performance. Curiosity softens rigidity and creates room for new possibilities.

Old wiring loops automatically. Avoidance is only the beginning. Clarity arrives when we recognize the patterns shaping perception and bring them into the light—not to judge them but to see them clearly. Once named, these distortions lose authority. The script is interrupted, choice is reclaimed, and autopilot gives way to mindful agency.

Thought Distortions: The Narrator's Greatest Hits

Your brain's narrator rarely reports the news as it is. Instead, it offers commentary. Sometimes it sounds like a doom-laden Nostradamus prophecy, predicting disaster with every play. Other times, it plays the cautious planner, stockpiling emotional defenses against pain, risk, and disappointment.

Its intention is often protection, not sabotage. The problem is that it does not deliver facts—it tells stories. And those stories shape how we see ourselves, others, and the world.

Thought distortions are some of the narrator's greatest hits. They warp perspective, invite fear, and amplify self-doubt. Recognizing them is the first step to reclaiming choice.

Catastrophizing: End-of-the-World Thinking

Catastrophizing is the classic worst-case-scenario distortion. A missed call becomes rejection. A canceled dinner feels like a verdict on your worth. A piece of feedback spirals into a full-blown crisis. The brain's narrator does not just jump to conclusions—it scripts disasters, complete with imagined consequences and dramatic replays.

It can feel protective: if the worst is already imagined, disappointment may sting less. But living in constant crisis mode warps perception. Small inconveniences swell into existential threats, minor mistakes feel like proof of failure, and the nervous system stays on high alert. Context disappears. Nuance collapses.

Grounding begins by questioning the story. Ask: Is this actually true? What evidence do I have? Could there be another explanation? Often, reality is simpler—the dinner was canceled because someone was sick, not because of you. The feedback was meant to guide, not condemn. The missed call had nothing to do with your value.

Catastrophizing is not a character flaw; it is a survival habit. The goal is not to fight the thought, but to meet it with curiosity. Notice the story, name it, and check it against reality. Over time, this practice loosens the grip of constant crisis thinking, turning inner drama into a signal you can respond to rather than be ruled by.

The Story or the Fact

When emotion surges, what are you reacting to—the situation, or the story about it? Curiosity—not certainty—creates space for what is actually true.

All-or-Nothing Thinking: The Tyranny of Absolutes

All-or-nothing thinking is the distortion that reduces life to extremes. If a day is not perfect, it is ruined. If an effort is not flawless, it is a failure. The brain's narrator favors absolutes because they feel safe. They simplify decisions, reduce uncertainty, and create the illusion of control. The cost of that safety, however, is high.

Life is rarely either/or; it is almost always both/and. A meeting may be awkward and still productive. A project may be flawed and still meaningful. A relationship may be messy and still loving. All-or-nothing thinking erases these complexities, turning ordinary imperfections into final judgments.

This distortion fuels a rigid, perfection-driven mindset. It teaches that partial effort is meaningless, mistakes are unforgivable, and compromise signals weakness. Over time, it produces chronic dissatisfaction, heightened anxiety, and a persistent sense of falling short—often in direct conflict with reality.

Awareness softens its grasp. Recognizing all-or-nothing thinking allows life to regain texture. Progress becomes visible without demanding mastery. Growth may be uneven and uncomfortable, but it remains real. Releasing the tyranny of absolutes restores freedom: the ability to live in nuance, honor effort, and find meaning in imperfection rather than despair.

Overgeneralizing: One Event, Lifetime Sentence

Overgeneralizing is the distortion that turns a single event into a sweeping verdict on life. One mistake becomes proof that you will always fail. One disappointment becomes evidence that nothing will ever work out. The brain's narrator thrives on these extremes, weaving always and never into the inner dialogue:

I always mess this up.
No one ever notices.
Everything I try fails.

These statements reveal how the mind stretches one moment into a lifetime sentence. Overgeneralizing erases context, complexity, and perspective. It treats exceptions as irrelevant and paints reality with a single, unforgiving brushstroke. A missed deadline is not evidence of chronic incompetence. A criticism is not a prophecy of universal rejection.

This distortion is seductive because it simplifies the world. It offers a clear, if inaccurate, storyline where cause and effect feel neat and predictable. The cost, however, is steep: discouragement, self-doubt, and the quiet erosion of resilience. When one event is treated as permanent, momentum stalls and fear of failure takes over.

The antidote is conscious recognition. Noticing overgeneralization allows each experience to exist on its own terms rather than as a prediction of destiny. It invites curiosity: Is this truly always the case? What exceptions exist? What alternative perspectives are being ignored? By questioning sweeping conclusions, choice and agency return.

Overgeneralizing does not disappear overnight. It is a habitual lens reinforced over time. But noticing it, questioning it, and gently redirecting thought patterns restores movement. Life becomes moment-to-moment again. Mistakes become information, not verdicts. Possibility reappears where certainty once closed the door.

Filtering: The Negativity Magnifier

Filtering is the mental distortion that magnifies the negative while muting the positive. The brain's narrator favors this trick. One critique outweighs ten compliments. One difficult moment eclipses an otherwise good day. Filtering disguises itself as vigilance—as if scanning for flaws keeps you safe—but its real effect is narrowed perspective and diminished joy.

This distortion persists because the brain is wired to notice threat. Evolutionarily, danger detection supported survival. In modern life, however, that same hyper-alertness often turns inward. A minor criticism becomes evidence of incompetence. An awkward interaction is interpreted as social failure. Meanwhile, moments of success, cooperation, or kindness are minimized, dismissed, or forgotten altogether.

Over time, filtering reshapes experience. A day filled with progress and connection can feel flat or disappointing because a single mistake dominates the narrative. Anxiety increases. Irritability follows. Satisfaction erodes. The mind becomes a magnifying glass for what went wrong while what went right fades into the background.

The antidote is deliberate attention. Noticing the filter in action restores balance. Achievements are acknowledged alongside mistakes. Feedback is placed in context. The story becomes fuller, more accurate, and less punitive. This is not forced optimism or denial—it is expanded perception. Filtering does not disappear instantly, but awareness paired with intentional noticing softens its hold, restores depth, and allows joy to return to focus.

Personalization: The Self-Blame Loop

Personalization is the mental distortion that assumes everything is about you. The brain's narrator eagerly constructs these stories. A colleague's silence becomes evidence of anger directed at you. A friend's canceled plans are quietly interpreted as your fault. A minor mistake by someone else is reframed as proof that you somehow caused it. Personalization assigns responsibility where none exists, layering guilt, anxiety, and unnecessary self-reproach.

This distortion feels compelling because it offers the illusion of control. If everything hinges on your actions, then changing yourself appears to promise a different outcome. In reality, it is a trap. The world does not revolve around you, and most events are shaped by variables entirely outside your influence. Internalizing responsibility for external circumstances creates a self-perpetuating cycle of blame and emotional overexertion (Laney, 2002).

The consequences accumulate quietly. Personalization erodes confidence, fuels chronic worry, and distorts relationships. Apologies multiply. Interactions are overanalyzed. Neutral behaviors are scanned for hidden meaning. Life becomes a constant decoding exercise, where every glance, pause, or tone is treated as a referendum on your worth.

The antidote is gentle curiosity. Pause and ask whether the situation truly centers on you or if other explanations exist. Perhaps the colleague is distracted. Perhaps the friend is overwhelmed. Perhaps nothing is being communicated at all. By stepping back, naming the distortion, and considering alternative interpretations, the self-blame loop loosens its grip.

Personalization patterns are rarely undone in a moment. Awareness transforms it from a relentless internal critic into a useful signal—informative rather than accusatory. It creates enough space for emotion to settle, perspective to return, and response to replace overreaction.

Should Statements: The Invisible Burden

Few words carry as much weight as *should*. The brain's narrator slips it in effortlessly, whether turned inward (*I should be further along. I should be better. I should have done more*) or outward (*They should appreciate me. They should behave differently*). *Should* disguises judgment as motivation. It masquerades as guidance while quietly feeding comparison, self-imposed ideals, and guilt.

This distortion works because *should* implies a universal standard—a rigid measure of success, morality, or worth. It positions the mind as both judge and jury, creating an internal courtroom where the verdict is nearly always guilty. Every deviation from these imagined rules becomes evidence of inadequacy. Every unmet expectation becomes a personal failure.

Living under the tyranny of *should* erodes satisfaction and self-respect. It convinces you that progress is insufficient, effort is never enough, and other people's behavior is yours to manage or correct—even when it is not. *Should* narrows perception, turning life into a checklist of obligations rather than a lived experience.

The antidote is conscious choice. Reframing *should* into curiosity, possibility, or value-driven intention transforms pressure into agency. Ask yourself: Do I want to do this? Does this align with what matters to me? What changes if I approach this with intention instead of obligation? Growth does not thrive under rigid rules. It emerges through awareness, alignment, and deliberate choice.

Recognizing *should* statements is not about abandoning standards or responsibility. It is about reclaiming freedom. By noticing when *should* appears, naming it, and choosing intentionally, you loosen the invisible burden and create space for flexibility, clarity, and genuine satisfaction.

From "Should" to Chosen

What "should" has been quietly draining your energy?
Whose standard is it—yours, someone else's, or the world's?
Rewrite it as a choice. Feel how your agency returns.

Unclenching Your Brain: From Awareness to Action

Naming the distortions—the DMN's favorite tricks—gives you choice. Awareness interrupts the automatic script, but it does not erase it. The inner narrator still speaks; the difference is that you now decide whether to listen. Unclenching your brain means loosening the grip of fear and habit, observing thoughts without being captured by them, and choosing which stories deserve your energy.

Every action has consequences, including unintended ones. Yet often it is inaction—avoidance, denial, numbing—that exacts the highest cost. Fear, rejection, and failure rarely come from boldness. They come from shrinking. From ghosting your own needs. From ignoring the emotional closets where old stories and unprocessed feelings wait. Self-determination is not a single decision; it is thousands of small choices—conscious instead of automatic, curious instead of defensive, honest instead of rehearsed.

Your thoughts shape perception. Perception filters reality. Reality becomes the ground on which you build your life. A mental lens colored by mistrust or unhealed wounds turns experience into a self-fulfilling prophecy. You react instead of respond. You protect instead of connect. You repeat rather than grow.

Freedom begins when you stop performing and start being. It is the ability to pause, feel, and choose deliberately. Each time you notice a distortion, each time you reclaim authority over a thought, you are practicing self-determination. The narrator in your head works for you—not the other way around. You can edit. You can delete. You can rewrite.

Noise to North Star

Once you reclaim authority over your mind, a new question emerges: What guides that authority? What actually matters to you—not what society, your parents, or your peers say should matter; not the borrowed metrics of success, popularity, or approval—but what you would stand for if no one were watching. What you would protect. What you would return to when the noise finally fades.

Releasing old narratives and quieting distortions is only the beginning. The next step is intentional choice. Identifying what matters most. Naming your non-negotiables. Defining the principles you will not trade—even when doing so costs comfort, certainty, or approval.

Values are both anchor and compass: the quiet, unshakable foundation beneath the chaos. They point the way forward when fear speaks loudly, when pressure mounts, when conformity is rewarded. And that steady inner knowing—the part of you that recognizes truth without explanation—that is the voice worth following.

Without values, clarity drifts. The world's noise steps in as a substitute compass, and even hard-won freedom loses direction. Without a North Star, calm can feel confusing, and open skies strangely unsteady.

That is where we go next—into the work of knowing your values, living them unapologetically, and allowing them to shape not only your choices but your energy, your relationships, and the legacy you leave behind.

Your values are already there. It is time to listen.

From Noise to North Star

Quiet the Echo

Which old narratives still try to echo in your mind—and
which are finally losing their hold?
Peace begins when you stop arguing with noise and start
listening for what remains steady.

Truth in Stillness

What truth remains when the noise finally softens?
Stillness does not erase districation—it reveals the
signal that has been there all along.

Follow the Compass

When your mind grows quiet, what values rise the the
surface? Your truth does not shout—it points. Listen closely.
Your North Star is already guiding you home.

Chapter 5:
Know What You Value (Or You Will Fall for Anything)

From Presence to Alignment

Knowing your worth matters, but living from it is where real transformation begins. That shift happens when self-loyalty moves from belief into practice—when you show up present, aware, and aligned with what you value. This is the bridge between understanding your worth and embodying it.

When you live this way, your energy changes. It stops being transactional and becomes grounded. Others feel it, even if they cannot explain why. Your confidence does not announce itself; it settles the room. You stop merely surviving circumstances and begin responding to them with intention. As your standards rise, your life follows.

Showing up fully is not performative. It is consistency. It is courage. It is choosing alignment over appeasement and clarity over chaos. Each interaction becomes an expression of self-respect. You stop bending to expectations and start honoring your truth.

This is where insight meets pressure. Understanding your worth is one thing; inhabiting it in real time—through uncertainty, tension, and imperfect moments—is another. How do you stay grounded when stress escalates? How do you remain aligned when expectations collide? How do you show up without abandoning yourself? This is where presence becomes power.

The Compass Within

Presence anchors you in the moment; values give that moment meaning. Together, they form the quiet coordinates of integrity and resonant leadership.

Knowing your worth begins with knowing what you value. Without that clarity, life becomes reactive. You start saying yes to what looks good, only to realize later that it does not sustain you. Time, energy, and attention drift toward other people's priorities and your own begin to blur.

Values function as an internal navigation system. Without them, you wander—pulled by distraction, persuasion, and urgency. With them, you move with quiet certainty. You recognize dead ends disguised as opportunity. You avoid compromises that cost your peace. Your path becomes deliberate, grounded, and unmistakably your own.

Values translate presence into alignment, self-awareness into action, and intention into choice.

Alignment is not perfection; it is congruence. It is living in a way where thoughts, words, and actions point in the same direction— where your inner compass matches your outward life. When alignment is present, life stops feeling like a tug-of-war between obligation and desire and begins moving with the steady pull of your principles.

Clarifying your values is not abstract or philosophical. It is practical. It is the foundation of emotional freedom, sound decision-making, and personal power. Values act as internal signals, guiding you toward a life lived with intention rather than reaction.

And this is the quiet shift: when you live from your values, everything changes. Your energy steadies. Your decisions simplify. Your relationships recalibrate. You move with discernment instead of urgency and resonance instead of performance. Life becomes less about managing impressions and more about honoring your own compass.

So, pause. Reflect. Identify what truly matters—not what earns approval, not what looks impressive, not what others expect.

Know your standards.
Claim your priorities.
Let your values guide every choice, boundary, and step.

The Power in Naming

List five values that anchor you—such as honesty, growth, compassion, courage, and peace. Name them, know them, embrace them. Words give conviction and power.
What you name, you can stand on.

The Deep Architecture of Values

Your values form the deep architecture of who you are. They are not surface-level preferences or fleeting desires. Values live beneath habit, expectation, and performance—rooted in both conscious intention and unconscious patterns. They are not cravings that fade once the spotlight moves nor ideals that sound admirable until they require sacrifice. Integrity that disappears under pressure is not a value. Balance preached while burnout is glorified is not alignment.

Values are the quiet infrastructure beneath every thought, choice, and relationship. They are what remain when titles, achievements, and external validation are stripped away.

True values do not shift with circumstance; they reveal themselves through it. They become most visible when pressure rises—when pleasing others feels tempting, when performance is rewarded, when bending would be easier than standing firm. In those moments, values act as an internal framework, holding your integrity upright when compromise calls your name.

Values function as both lens and compass. They shape how you interpret the world and guide how you move through it. When you know them, your actions arise from intention rather than impulse. You begin to understand why certain environments drain you, why some opportunities energize you, and why certain relationships feel heavy while others feel steady. Your instincts stop feeling confusing; they become clear signals aligned with your inner structure.

Values bring order to your emotional landscape. They turn chaos into coherence, reactivity into insight, and confusion into grounded action.

Consider a manager who values honesty over comfort. When a costly error surfaces, they address it directly instead of protecting appearances. That single choice—truth over avoidance—builds trust, stabilizes culture, and demonstrates values in motion.

Or consider a parent who values presence over obligation, choosing to decline a late work request in order to attend a child's recital. The decision reinforces both boundaries and priorities, without apology.

Anchored in your values, life shifts. Performance-driven rhythms give way to integrity, presence, and alignment. You make choices that honor both your energy and your truth—even when the world is loud, urgent, or demanding.

Values allow you to move through life with confidence, knowing the course you chart is yours. Not dictated by trends, opinions, or expectations. They transform daily living from survival into intention, from reaction into self-respect.

The Value You Don't Negotiate

Which value holds steady even when comfort wavers? Which one do you quietly bargain away when things get hard? The distance between the two reveals where growth is asking to happen.

Values as Your Emotional North Star

Values are the quiet code running beneath everything you do. They shape how you respond under pressure, how you prioritize your time, and how you carry yourself when no one is watching. Long before anyone else notices or approves, your values are already guiding your choices. In a world saturated with noise, urgency, and distraction, they provide steadiness—anchoring you when uncertainty feels overwhelming.

When life's storms arrive—tight deadlines, conflict, instability, or unexpected loss—values function as stabilizers. They clarify which battles are worth engaging, which compromises erode your integrity, and what truly deserves your energy. Even the smallest decisions—how you spend an hour, which invitations you accept, which opportunities you decline—quietly reveal what you stand for. Without this clarity, subtle compromises accumulate, leading to quiet exhaustion, tension, and drift. With it, each choice becomes an act of alignment—an expression of who you are and what you will not surrender.

Values also guide you through life's gray areas. When outcomes are uncertain and choices are imperfect, they keep your energy focused on what genuinely matters rather than scattering it across expectations, obligations, or pressures that were never yours to carry.

Understanding your values is not a one-time insight; it is an ongoing practice. As you grow, refine, and shed old identities, your values continue to orient you. Once named, they become a reliable internal compass—shaping priorities, strengthening relationships, and infusing decisions with purpose. They offer a steady reference point, helping you remain grounded even when external forces try to pull you off course.

Your values do not shout. They point.
And when the noise rises, they are what guide you home.

Living Your Values in Real Time

Theory is easy. Life is not.

Knowing your values is one thing; living them within the unpredictable rhythm of daily life is another. It is simple to articulate what matters when conditions are calm. The real test appears in motion—when the inbox overflows, the meeting runs long, or someone's energy pulls you off balance. That is when values move from concept into practice. They stop being words on a page and start becoming choices that either reinforce or erode your integrity.

Values serve as an internal compass, but they are also a daily invitation—to emotional awareness, honesty, and action. Each day offers countless moments to translate what you value into how you speak, what you prioritize, and how you treat others. Alignment happens in micro-moments: saying no to what drains you, speaking when silence would betray your principles, choosing rest instead of equating worth with productivity.

Living in alignment is rarely one decisive act. It is the accumulation of small, deliberate choices repeated over time. Every yes and every no either strengthens or weakens the bridge between who you are and how you live. Over time, those choices create a recognizable steadiness—one that others feel before you ever speak.

Consistency is what turns values into credibility. When your actions reflect your principles day after day, trust forms naturally. Not because you never falter, but because you return to alignment again and again. That steadiness becomes magnetic. You stop reacting to circumstances and start responding from something deeper than emotion or urgency.

Living your values is not about declaring them. It is about embodying them. Your tone carries the message. Your posture delivers the proof. Integrity does not need performance; it radiates. It shows up in the boundaries you hold, the calm you bring into conflict, and the clarity you maintain under pressure.

This is what it means to live your values in real time: allowing them to guide decisions, protect energy, and steady attention. External pressure loses its authority. Expression replaces reaction.

When you live this way, you lead this way. Responding to misalignment—internal or external—with quiet emotional steadiness is leadership in motion. People notice when words and actions match, when boundaries remain firm and humane, and when presence stays grounded even in tension. Integrity becomes visible without explanation.

Values simplify decisions. You can meet a request, invitation, or opportunity with a single question:

Does this align with what I say I value?

If the answer is no, that is sufficient. No guilt. No justification. No mental gymnastics.

Values shape the tone of your presence.

If growth matters, you move toward what expands you and step away from what diminishes you. If compassion guides you, you invest in relationships rooted in mutual care and release those built on depletion.

When values lead, choice becomes aligned.
Habit loosens its grip.
Obligation fades.
Truth takes the wheel.

The Boundaries That Protect What You Value

Boundaries are the physical and emotional expression of what you value. They are not walls meant to exclude; they are lines of respect that define the conditions for safety, mutual regard, and authenticity. **A clear boundary says, "This is how I protect what matters most."** It is an act of self-respect that keeps your values intact. Saying no, stepping back, or naming what is not acceptable is not rejection. It is reverence—for yourself and for the kind of relationships you intend to sustain.

A professional may decline a last-minute request that encroaches on family time. A friend may quietly exit a conversation that repeatedly crosses an emotional line. In both cases, the boundary communicates clarity rather than conflict and care rather than control. It honors self without devaluing others.

When boundaries are grounded in values, they stop feeling like defenses. They become expressions of integrity—communicated calmly, consistently, and without excess explanation. Boundaries do not require justification because they are lived, not debated. Those who respect you will adapt. Those who do not will distance themselves. Either way, your peace remains intact.

Life will always present competing priorities: work and family, ambition and rest, principle and pressure. In those moments, values become your compass. The pause before choosing turns into sacred space. You ask yourself: Does this align with who I am becoming? Does this honor my integrity, energy, and relationships?

Choices made from this place feel different. Life shifts from reaction to creation. Energy is conserved for what matters. Attention stops scattering where it does not belong.

Living from your values is a practice of intention. It requires noticing when you drift and returning—gently, deliberately—to alignment. With practice, boundaries stop feeling restrictive and start feeling liberating. Decisions lose their weight and gain clarity.

Over time, something powerful occurs. Your words, energy, and actions begin to harmonize. You move through life with quiet confidence—not because everything is easy, but because you are anchored. People feel that steadiness when they encounter you, and trust forms naturally.

Values are not abstract ideals or moral slogans. They are living tools—flexible, clarifying, and deeply human. They shape how you connect, how you decide, and how you lead. When you live them fully, your life becomes not only successful but meaningful.

Your Calendar Tells the Truth

If someone studied only your calendar, what would they assume you value most? If that story feels untrue, begin rewriting the evidence—one choice, one boundary at a time.
Your time speaks before your words ever do.

Recognizing and Responding to Misalignment

Living your values in real time requires attention to subtle signals. The twinge of unease when someone interrupts, the irritation when a process feels unfair, the quiet fatigue after a particular conversation—these are not disruptions. They are guideposts. They reveal where your energy, attention, or boundaries are being compromised.

Misalignment is information, not judgment.

It invites correction before small compromises harden into patterns and resentment becomes a way of living.

Noticing misalignment is as important as responding to it. Pausing to reflect—asking why something felt off, which value was challenged, and what response would honor both your integrity and your peace— creates the foundation for intentional living. With practice, this reflection becomes instinctive. Your values begin to operate like an internal radar, guiding responses toward alignment rather than reactivity (Kolb, 1984).

Misalignment does not exist only within you. It appears in relationships, teams, and families. It is inevitable. People change.

Circumstances shift. Priorities evolve. The goal is not to eliminate tension but to recognize it, interpret it accurately, and respond deliberately.

The signals are rarely dramatic. They whisper; discomfort in conversation, exhaustion after certain interactions, recurring frustration around specific decisions, unease when commitments clash with your principles. These quiet cues are your compass, pointing toward what needs attention.

When trust is a core value, a colleague who repeatedly overpromises and underdelivers triggers more than irritation—it signals misalignment. When integrity grounds you, tolerating silent shortcuts drains energy over time. These moments are not inconveniences. They are alerts.

Approach misalignment without judgment. Differences in values are not failures; they are realities. Diverse perspectives and priorities are part of being human. Misalignment simply reveals where your truth diverges from someone else's. Curiosity allows you to navigate that divergence with clarity rather than defensiveness.

When you pause long enough to interpret the signal instead of silencing it, groundedness returns. Reaction gives way to response. The next right step becomes visible. Intentional action begins in the quiet space between awareness and choice.

The Quiet Compass

Where in your life do you keep feeling "off," even when everything looks fine on paper? That discomfort is not dysfunction—it is direction. Misalignment is not asking for judgment;
it is asking for honesty.

When misalignment appears—and it will—your values give you three clear options: adapt, communicate, or exit. Each requires emotional regulation and courage. You are not required to react. You are allowed to choose.

Sometimes the right response is adaptation. This means adjusting your approach without abandoning your principles. Flexibility is not self-betrayal; it is strength. You can bend without breaking, evolve without erasing yourself, and remain aligned while navigating change.

At other times, intention calls for communication. This is the willingness to name what feels off—clearly, calmly, and without accusation. Grounded conversations rooted in honesty and curiosity can accomplish what avoidance never does: restore understanding, rebuild trust, and realign expectations before resentment takes hold.

And then there are moments when the most self-respecting choice is to step away. Exiting is not failure. It is self-loyalty in action. It is recognizing that staying, in some situations, costs more than leaving ever will. Walking away honors both your peace and your values when compromise becomes erosion.

There is no universally correct response. Adaptation, communication, and exit are all valid. The right choice is the one that preserves your integrity and keeps you aligned with who you are becoming.

The Next Right Step

Which situations in your life are asking you to adapt, communicate, or exit? Which response would honor both your integrity and your peace? Courage is not reacting. Courage is choosing with clarity.

Alignment between what you say you value and how you actually live is the true measure of authenticity—and it is how others assess your trustworthiness. Reflection is the bridge between intention and embodiment. Without it, even the most meaningful values remain abstract: admirable in theory, but hollow in practice.

Reflection is not self-judgment; it is awareness. It allows you to notice drift before disconnection becomes habit. The goal is not perfection, but consciousness—the ability to recognize when your choices, priorities, or tone begin to move away from your internal compass. Reflection prevents drift. It translates vague discomfort into clarity and turns awareness into aligned action (Kolb, 1984).

Reflection does not require long retreats or elaborate rituals. It lives in the pauses between responsibilities: a walk after a demanding day, a quiet drive, a measured breath before a meeting. The measure of reflection is honesty, not duration. Ask whether that interaction reflected who you intend to be, what your frustration reveals about what you value, or which patterns surface when priorities are ignored.

Each question draws you back into alignment, creating a dialogue between intention, emotion, and behavior. That dialogue becomes recalibration. The rhythm is simple: reflect, recalibrate, recommit. Over time, this cycle strengthens integrity and steadies confidence, shifting authenticity from performance to presence.

Values are not static; they evolve as you do. Reflection keeps your internal compass accurate, allowing you to meet change without losing yourself. In time, reflection becomes less about correction and more about trust—the grounded confidence that your life is aligned from the inside out.

Aligning with Your North Star

Approach these prompts with curiosity, not criticism. Let reflection become movement—awareness translated into deliberate action.

Anchor Points

What three values feel most essential to who you are right now? How do they show up—or fail to show up—in your daily choices?

Alignment Check

Where do you feel most congruent with your values? Where do you sense friction, and what might that tension be teaching you?

Boundaries and Energy

Which environments or relationships nourish your values? Which ones quietly pull you away from them?

Courage in Action

Recall a moment when you compromised a value. What did it cost you—emotionally or energetically? How might you respond differently next time?

Integration

Name one small action this week that would bring you closer to alignment with what you value. What will you need to release or decline to honor that choice?

This process is less about doing it a prescribed way and more about being present with yourself. Each reflection strengthens your ability to live with intention and integrity. The more often you return to your values, the more naturally they guide your choices, shape your relationships, and steady your peace.

A Bridge to Self-Worth

Values clarify direction. Worth defines your readiness to walk in that direction. Once you are anchored in your values, your inner compass naturally points toward worth.

Understanding your worth is not about ego, arrogance, or comparison. It is about recognizing the inherent value of your time, energy, and presence. Values tell you where to go; worth tells you what is worth traveling for. When your life reflects your principles, the question of what you will accept—and what you will no longer tolerate—becomes unmistakably clear.

Think of values as the compass. They guide alignment, authenticity, and integrity. Worth is the terrain. It defines the boundaries you will not cross, the obstacles you refuse to normalize, and the paths you will no longer wander. Together, they provide both direction and foundation, allowing you to move through life with intention rather than reaction.

When you live in alignment with your values, your relationships, commitments, and emotional investments begin to mirror your intrinsic worth. You stop performing for approval. You stop bending to expectations. You stop settling for less than respect. Boundaries cease to be negotiations and become natural expressions of who you are and what you deserve. When you act from worth, your energy speaks first—calm, clear, and steady.

Values and worth are inseparable partners. Values guide the journey; worth sets the limits and the pace. Together, they form the root system of authentic confidence—the kind that moves quietly yet unmistakably through every decision, interaction, and space you occupy.

Anchored in both, you begin to operate from grounded self-assurance: deliberate, centered, and clear. The next step is embodiment—to live your worth through self-respect, steady leadership, and emotional boundaries. This is the bridge from knowing who you are to living it—fully, unapologetically, and with grounded power.

When you know what you value and live accordingly, you stop chasing every shiny distraction and begin rising in alignment with the people, environments, and opportunities meant for you.

The Worth You Stand On

When values show you the way, worth determines how far you go. The next step is not merely knowing you are enough—it is deciding, leading, and loving as if you believe it.

Because worth, when lived, is not a declaration.
It is a standard.

Stand in Your Values

Worth Has Standards

What treatment is no longer acceptable for you, specifically?
What boundary would protect that standard next time it is
tested? Standing in your values does not require apology.

Gatekeeping Your Energy

Which commitments still reflect your values but no longer
honor your worth? What will you pause, delegate, or release
this month to reclaim peace? And how will you protect that
reclaimed energy from being quietly absorbed again?

Align to Advance

Which value will guide your next decision?
What boundary will keep it intact when challenged?
What one sentence will you use this week to protect your
alignment when pressure rises?

Chapter 6:
Understand Your Worth (It Is Not Up for Debate)

Where Worth Begins

Understanding your worth begins with knowing what you value. Values guide your choices; worth determines what you will tolerate. Values are not abstract ideals—they are the internal compass that informs every boundary, decision, and interaction. Worth is the terrain you navigate with that compass.

Your worth is your responsibility to steward. It is not the job of your partner, boss, or friends. It belongs solely to you.

Your task is to discover it, nurture it, and protect it with unwavering conviction. Just as your inner narrative shapes how you see yourself, your values define what you stand for—together, they form the foundation of genuine self-worth.

Here is what becomes undeniable: once you genuinely recognize your value, you stop arguing with people who never intended to understand you. You stop seeking recognition from those still searching for their own. Worth does not require witnesses; it requires self-awareness and alignment with your values.

Awareness of your worth changes how you move through life. It shapes your decisions, your boundaries, and how you invest your energy. When your actions reflect what you truly value, leaving situations or relationships that no longer serve you becomes an act of growth, not drama. Growth often requires releasing jobs, relationships, conversations, or identities once used to earn acceptance.

Reclaiming What You Gave Away

Where have you traded your worth for someone else's approval? Each time you refuse to negotiate your value, you reclaim a part of yourself that was never theirs to hold.

Claiming Your Worth in Motion

Letting go is not rejection—it is evolution. It is alignment and maturity in motion. It is the moment you choose truth over attachment and integrity over comfort, creating space for what is true to begin.

Consider the professional who repeatedly volunteers for extra work, hoping to prove value to a manager who rarely acknowledges it. The day they stop offering is not rebellion—it is reclamation. By setting a boundary, they make room for work that energizes, challenges, and aligns with their values. This is not about doing less. It is about honoring more.

Acknowledging your inherent worth releases the need to explain, justify, or defend yourself. You no longer have to rationalize your feelings, choices, or priorities. You simply exist—and that is enough. This is quiet liberation. As external validation fades, your inner compass takes the lead. Decisions sharpen. Boundaries strengthen. Priorities clarify. Your life begins to reflect your values in motion.

Worth is not earned through productivity or popularity. It is intrinsic. It is immovable. Recognizing it requires turning inward—away from noise, judgment, and comparison—toward the quiet signals of self-respect and alignment.

When you claim your worth fully, the world adjusts. Friction often follows—not because you are wrong, but because old dynamics are recalibrating. Relationships, opportunities, and environments shift. Those aligned with your integrity remain. Others drift away. This is not loss—it is truth coming into focus. You begin moving from grounded self-assurance rather than performance.

Understanding your worth is not a single realization. It is a practice—choosing truth over approval again and again until it becomes how you live.

This is where knowing your worth becomes living it. It appears in small, deliberate acts: declining what drains you, speaking when it matters, protecting your peace without apology. Each choice becomes an act of self-loyalty—a quiet declaration that says I matter.

Worth is not a concept to admire. It is a force to embody. When you act from it, your presence shifts. You stop chasing belonging—you create it.

The Wrong Ruler

List three external measures you have used as proof of your worth. Which will you retire first?

Do Not Shrink. Do Not Puff. Just Stand

There is a profound difference between loudness and confidence. Confidence is not measured by volume, audience size, or force of opinion. It is not determined by agreement, applause, or visibility. True confidence is quiet, grounded, and anchored in self-trust (Johnston, McKee, & Boyatzis, 2008). It shows up as composure in tension, discernment about which conversations deserve energy, and the ability to pause rather than perform.

Confidence does not demand recognition or validation. It does not seek to persuade others of its legitimacy. It simply exists—contained, steady, and self-assured. Loudness, by contrast, is often insecurity dressed as certainty. Noise masquerading as power shouts to be seen because silence feels like invisibility. Real power does not need an audience. It holds.

True confidence is responsive, not reactive. It does not rise and fall with opinion or circumstance. It allows you to leave what no longer fits without explanation or bitterness. It recognizes when something has served its purpose and steps away with dignity (Kishimi & Koga, 2013). Confidence speaks through behavior, not declaration. It moves with restraint, clarity, and calm. It signals, without drama, "This is no longer mine"—and it leaves in peace.

Standing fully in who you are commands respect without demanding it. Choosing honesty, self-regard, and integrity may unsettle those accustomed to your compliance. When you stop minimizing yourself for others' comfort, their discomfort becomes information—not a cue to retreat. Authenticity reveals where others may still be hiding, and not everyone welcomes that mirror.

Do not shrink to be digestible. Do not inflate yourself to be noticed. Stand—quietly, firmly, fully. Stand in self-awareness. Stand in truth. Stand in the space between reaction and restraint, where real strength lives. Boundaries are part of that stance. They are not walls, but doors—clear, intentional, and grounded in mutual respect.

Peace is not passive. It does not require enduring disrespect or suppressing discomfort to maintain appearances. Peace comes from knowing where you stand, what you allow, and what no longer belongs in your orbit. Consider where peace and avoidance may have merged—where silence protected comfort instead of truth. Your calm becomes communication, speaking more clearly than defensiveness ever could.

Standing tall—neither shrinking nor posturing—is a radical act of self-loyalty. Do not shrink. Do not puff. Just stand. This is grounded confidence—unshaken, unprovoked, and undistracted by noise.

Confidence is quiet.
When paired with self-respect, it becomes unshakable.

Standing All the Way Up

*Where do you still feel the pull to shrink, perform, or prove?
What would change if you stood fully rooted in your values and
unafraid to take up the space your integrity requires?*

Follow Your Worth, Not Your Ego: Small Steps = Big Shifts

Ego shouts. Worth whispers. Ego is driven by proving and being seen. Worth does not require an audience. Ego seeks validation; worth acts from alignment. True confidence begins when you stop chasing approval and start living from the value already within you.

Outgrowing people, roles, or patterns is not arrogance—it is evolution. Worth guides that evolution by clarifying what you allow, how you respond, and when it is time to release. You can walk away without explanation or applause. You can stop waiting for apologies that will never arrive. You do not owe explanations to those unwilling to understand you.

Leading from worth means leading from peace, not pride. It is releasing with clarity rather than resentment. Alignment speaks louder than ego. The most powerful statement you can make is no longer needing to prove anything.

This quiet confidence redirects attention inward. Stop waiting to be understood. Start understanding yourself—your patterns, triggers, and emotional reflexes. Growth begins there.

Align your energy with what you value, not what you fear. Invest in people, spaces, and work that expand you. Editing yourself to keep the peace only creates inner conflict. Your worth is not a group project. The version of you that once settled had reasons. The version standing here now has clarity.

Clarity does not shout. It chooses. It redirects. It releases. Growth arrives through small, deliberate acts: an honest conversation, a pause before reacting, a boundary that protects peace. Each act quietly declares alignment over approval.

When you live this way, you stop chasing belonging—it finds you. The people and environments meant for you meet you at your level of self-respect. Others fall away. That is not loss. It is liberation.

Alignment is power.
Peace is proof.

Which Voice Leads

When decisions arise, which voice speaks first—ego's urgency or worth's calm? One seeks validation. The other preserves peace. Which one are you following today?

The Cost of Self-Neglect

Understanding your worth and standing in grounded confidence is not a one-time achievement—it is a protective practice. When you honor your values and boundaries, you guard against the slow erosion that comes from outsourcing your sense of self. When confidence falters or worth is neglected, the consequences accumulate quietly, almost imperceptibly, until they become impossible to ignore.

Self-neglect rarely announces itself. It does not erupt—it seeps. When you rely on others—partners, workplaces, institutions—to define your value, you hand them the pen to write "enough" on your forehead. You contort, perform, shrink, or inflate yourself to meet expectations, drifting further from your internal compass. Red flags get ignored. Boundaries blur. Your own voice fades into static.

Society reinforces this. Self-abandonment can feel normal, particularly for those conditioned to equate worth with productivity or likability. Fitting in demands fragmentation; true belonging requires wholeness. You cannot build a home inside yourself if you are afraid to furnish it.

Eventually, the cost becomes visible. Trust in yourself erodes. Fatigue deepens. Emotional resilience thins. You wake up one day wondering how you strayed so far from yourself. Often, there was no dramatic trigger—just a quiet surrender of your inner authority, inch by inch.

Self-neglect infiltrates relationships, work, and your inner life. Conflict avoidance, indecision, chronic over-functioning—these are not character flaws; they are signals urging you back to yourself.

Recognition is empowerment. Once you see it, you can rebuild trust with yourself—honoring your needs, instincts, and truth. Saying no when it matters, pausing before reacting, choosing authenticity over performance—these are radical acts of self-loyalty. A single consistent boundary reminds you—and others—that your time, energy, and integrity are not negotiable.

This is not about guilt. It is about reclaiming your worth. Self-loyalty is integrity in motion. You cannot pour from an empty cup, and every decision rooted in worth compounds into authenticity and agency. Over time, these choices create a fortress of grounded self-command, where worth guides action and confidence becomes both shield and compass.

Small choices matter: declining a gathering that conflicts with your priorities, stepping back from a circular argument, choosing rest instead of relentlessly proving. They may look small on the outside; inside, they are seismic.

The cost of neglect is high. It shows up as exhaustion, chronic stress, blurred boundaries, and that persistent sense of being "off course." But the reward for reclaiming your worth is profound. Life responds differently. Opportunities align. Relationships deepen. Decisions sharpen. Your steadiness anchors you.

Protecting your worth is not indulgent—it is leadership. It is stewardship of your attention, your energy, your boundaries, and your voice. Each small act of alignment compounds into a life that is coherent and self-owned.

True confidence is quiet. It is demonstrated not in display but in the steadiness with which you navigate life guided by your values. Over time, consistency becomes magnetic. People trust how you show up because it is reliable, not because it is loud.

When your worth remains unclaimed, it does not simply distort how you see yourself—it distorts how you relate to others, limiting your capacity to engage authentically without losing yourself in the process (Cola & Wang, 2022).

Energy Tells the Truth

Which commitments fuel you—and which quietly drain you? This week, redistribute your focus toward what sustains your peace. Energy spent in alignment always returns as strength.

Becoming Visible to Yourself

The cost of self-neglect is not only internal—it quietly reshapes how you experience the world. When your worth goes unclaimed and recognition is delayed or denied, patterns emerge. You begin shrinking to fit spaces never designed for your full self. You over-function, over-give, and over perform, hoping effort will finally earn visibility.

Authenticity gets traded for approval. Self-abandonment disguises itself as service, and validation replaces genuine acknowledgment (Baumeister, 2001).

This is not simple validation-seeking. It is people-proving—the relentless attempt to convince the world (and often yourself) that you are enough, safe to love, and worthy of regard. The cost is substantial. You become the emotional stabilizer: resolving conflicts you did not create, managing emotions others never learned to hold, and carrying responsibilities that were never yours. You are essential in others' lives yet absent from your own. Empathy, attentiveness, generosity—the very qualities that make you remarkable—become camouflage. They help you belong while quietly erasing you.

Here is the unvarnished truth: No one is coming to hand you the recognition you were denied. That responsibility belongs to you now. You are the witness. The steady presence. The safe harbor you have been waiting for. Being unseen may be part of your history, but it does not define your future. You are allowed to take up space, express your needs, and rest without guilt. You are allowed to be layered, imperfect, and fully human—without earning it.

Visibility does not require confrontation or performance. It is quiet, steady, and unmistakable. When you stop chasing validation and start living in alignment, the world responds—not because you demand attention, but because you no longer disappear.

Becoming visible is a practice. It asks you to notice when you shrink, recognize when you perform, and choose—again and again—to stand in alignment with your own significance. Over time, your way of showing up becomes non-negotiable. Your energy becomes non-transferable. You become your own witness, advocate, and measure of worth.

What once felt like invisibility can become the foundation of deep self-recognition. Each time you speak truth, hold a boundary, or exist without apology, you revise the narrative. Small acts of self-loyalty accumulate into a life that is coherent, intentional, and fully yours.

And yet, reclaiming worth rarely begins with the outer world. It begins with unlearning the ways you were conditioned to abandon yourself in the name of love, loyalty, or responsibility.

Here is the quiet danger: self-neglect rarely announces itself. It disguises itself as helpfulness, generosity, dependability, or devotion. It wears the costume of good intentions and being needed. It can even be rewarded.

But beneath the surface, the exchange is uneven. You give until depleted, hoping someone will finally notice the cost. You call it compassion, but often it is compensation—a way to earn belonging that was never meant to require self-erasure.

This is where the story turns.

The drive to prove your worth and the habit of over-functioning often converge into one of the most socially praised—and personally damaging—identities of all: the Martyr.

Let us look closely at how self-abandonment masquerades as virtue, and how love—when distorted by exhaustion and overextension— quietly becomes sacrifice.

Visible Without Performing

Where have you shrunk or performed just to be seen?
What one small action today would honor your
presence without chasing approval? Visibility begins
the moment performance ends.

Exhibit A: The Martyr Complex Dressed as "Love"

Parenting is often wrapped in a guilt-soaked myth: Good parents sacrifice everything. Society glorifies exhaustion, but exhaustion is not noble—it is unsustainable.

Children matter, without question. But when a parent neglects rest, nourishment, and their own needs, the cost spreads. Operating from depletion is not parenting; it is survival. Love blurs into burnout. Self-abandonment gets mistaken for devotion.

Real love has boundaries. Caring for yourself is part of caring for others. Resting, saying no when depleted, or stepping back to regroup models wholeness. Children learn emotional regulation and self-respect more from example than instruction.

This pattern extends far beyond parenting to caregiving, leadership, and partnership. True love is sustainable. It is grounded. It honors integrity. Breaking the cycle requires deliberate choice: rest, reset, and model wholeness. Love is not self-erasure. It is showing up fully—human, responsible, and intact.

Exhibit B: Making Yourself Small—and Calling It Compromise

Without awareness of your worth, settling becomes easy. You tolerate neglect, remain in draining roles, or shrink to fit spaces never designed for you. You may call it maturity, flexibility, or teamwork. In reality, it is emotional self-erasure.

You anticipate needs, shape-shift to preserve harmony, and over-function to avoid conflict. Approval becomes conditional. Authenticity fades. You manage perception instead of inhabiting your truth.

Healthy relationships never require disappearance. Respect does not demand silence. Love does not ask you to shrink. Claim your voice. Speak plainly. Take up space without apology. Boundaries are not optional—they are foundational.

Shrinking for the comfort of others extracts a cost too high to sustain. Honoring your worth teaches the world how to meet you.

Exhibit C: You Attract What You Invite

Your internal standards shape what you allow. Low self-respect invites people and situations that confirm it. Conditioning may not be your fault—but recalibration is your responsibility.

Change the question. Not "Do they value me?" but "Are they worthy of me?" When your worth is clear, you stop chasing attention, bending to belong, or tolerating disregard. You evaluate relationships by mutuality, safety, and shared values.

You attract what mirrors how you treat yourself. Respect invites respect. Integrity draws integrity. There is no longer room for shrinking or accepting life as an afterthought.

Reclaim your space. Define what respect feels like. Enforce it—consistently.

Unmasking the Performance

Where have you been shrinking or over-functioning to meet expectations that were never yours? Whose approval are you still chasing? Liberation begins the moment you choose authenticity over applause.

Reclaiming Yourself: Love, Boundaries, and Worth

Taken together, the patterns revealed in Exhibits A-C (the martyr complex, self-erasure, and the energy you attract) point to a single truth: Reclaiming your worth requires conscious, deliberate action.

This work—setting boundaries, honoring your worth, and modeling wholeness—is not selfish. It is survival. It is leadership. It is love in its most authentic form. When you stop shrinking and performing and instead stand fully in your worth, you give others permission to do the same. You become a living blueprint for alignment, integrity, and grounded confidence. It is quiet power—but it is unmistakable.

When you stop expecting to be overlooked or undervalued, you stop tolerating it. How others treat you is rarely random; it often mirrors what you unconsciously believe you deserve. That sting you feel when dismissed or minimized is not weakness—it is information. A signal. A call to rise. Your worth was never something to earn. It has always been yours.

As you claim your worth and set clear standards, your energy shifts— from proving yourself to discerning what deserves your attention. You stop auditioning for acceptance. You begin observing instead of performing. People, situations, and environments that do not honor your value either adjust—or exit. Sometimes quietly. Sometimes with resistance. Either way, your inner compass sharpens. Your standards strengthen. Your presence becomes magnetic—not because you seek attention but because you honor yourself first.

This is not about harsh judgment or cutting people off. It is about discernment. You start noticing subtle cues: who drains your energy, who respects your boundaries, which patterns erode your integrity, and which choices align with who you are becoming. You stop settling. Your yeses carry intention. Your noes carry conviction. Life shifts from a series of uneasy compromises into an expression of conscious choice.

Borrowed Yeses

Which "yeses" in your life are truly yours—and which were issued from guilt, fear, or obligation? Every false yes drains integrity. Every honest no restores it.

When your standards rise, everything rises with you—your energy, your relationships, and your opportunities—aligning with the value you consistently honor. Each small act of self-loyalty—resting without guilt, saying no without explanation, walking away from draining dynamics, or choosing your energy over expectation—undoes old patterns and signals a life lived intentionally, on your own terms.

Martyrdom, codependency, shrinking, settling, and tolerating less than you deserve all trace back to one truth: your power was given away. Boundaries blurred. Value was outsourced. Situations were curated around a story you no longer need to live. None of this defines you. The cycle can end.

Healing does not come from approval, validation, or proving yourself. It begins with a decisive act: to choose yourself—consistently and unapologetically. Each boundary honored, each need prioritized, each misaligned attachment released restores your authority over your life.

This shift compounds. One small act of self-loyalty becomes a signal—to your nervous system, your relationships, and the world—that you operate from alignment rather than fear. Over time, those signals build a life that is coherent, resonant, and unmistakably your own.

The Worth Line

What single boundary could you assert today that would communicate—clearly and calmly—that your worth is non-negotiable? Even the smallest boundary, held with steadiness, becomes a declaration.

Showing up Fully: The Bridge from Self-Loyalty to Presence

Knowing your worth matters. Living from it is where transformation begins. That shift happens when self-loyalty becomes visible in real time—when you show up present, aware, and aligned with what you value. Worth stops being an idea you agree with and becomes a standard you embody.

When you live this way, your energy changes. It becomes steady. Others feel it even if they cannot name it. Your confidence does not need volume. It communicates through restraint, consistency, and the quiet clarity of someone who no longer negotiates their own integrity.

Showing up fully is not perfection. It is practice. It is choosing integrity over appeasement and authenticity over impression management. It is staying connected to yourself under pressure—when stress rises, expectations collide, and old patterns try to pull you back into shrinking, proving, or performing.

This is the bridge: self-worth lived as presence.

What follows is an exploration of how that presence actually lands—in rooms, conversations, conflict, and connection. Not in theory, but in the moment. In tone, posture, pacing, restraint, and silence. Because presence is not only what you feel inside—it is how others experience you.

Living Your Worth in Action

Sustain the Standard

What daily habit will help you sustain your worth an integrity? Worth is not just declared—it is practiced.

Honor over Proof

How will you remind yourself that your value was never something to prove—it was always something to honor? Your peace begins where performance ends.

Rise to Meet Yourself

What part of your life is ready to rise to the level of your worth—and what no longer fits that standard? Releasing what misaligns makes room for what already recognizes your value.

Part II: Showing Up — Presence, Listening, & Communication

You have done the inner work—or at least, you have begun.
You have quieted the noise, examined your reactions, softened where needed, and started treating yourself like someone who deserves care. That work matters. It is foundational.

But inner work only matters if it can be felt.

But now comes the translation.
The world cannot read your intentions.
It can only experience how you show up.

You can believe in empathy and still look perpetually irritated.
You can value respect and still interrupt mid-sentence.
You can be kind in theory and cutting in tone.

Most people are unaware of the gap between who they believe they are and how they are actually experienced.

This is where theory meets reality.

Where your energy, timing, tone, and facial expressions become part of your emotional résumé.
Where your silence communicates just as clearly as your words.
Where people decide—often subconsciously—whether they feel seen, safe, dismissed, or ignored.

Showing up with emotional intelligence means aligning intention with impact.

It means asking yourself:
- What shifts when I walk into the room?
- Who feels seen when I listen?
- What message do my micro-reactions send before my words even land?

This is not about proving your worth.
It is about honoring the moment.

It is where humility, courage, and emotional regulation intersect—and where trust quietly begins to grow.

Trust is not a title.
It is a feeling.

It is built in the calm response when frustration would be easier.
In the micro-moment you choose curiosity over defensiveness.
In the way consistency speaks louder than any declaration of integrity.

Every act of attentiveness, honesty, follow-through, and restraint compounds. Credibility grows through repetition—choice by choice, moment by moment.

This section is about that shift:
- From inner clarity to outer resonance
- From self-awareness to influence
- From knowing better to communicating better
- From meaning well to showing up well

Because how you show up is not a footnote.
It is the message.

Chapter 7:
How Do You Show Up? (Seriously, Take a Look)

"What you do makes a difference, and you have to decide what kind of difference you want to make."

— *Jane Goodall*

Your Presence Is Your Résumé

You are always showing up as something. Whether you realize it or not, you are broadcasting who you are—in every meeting, hallway conversation, email, sigh, and silence. What you know about your own worth becomes the lens through which you are experienced.

You enter the room before you speak. Your energy introduces you long before your words catch up. The question is not whether you are sending a message—it is which message you are sending.

This way of showing up is not passive. It is active, deliberate, and constantly communicating. It tells people more about you than any title ever could. From the moment you step into a space, people are reading your cues—the rhythm of your speech, the steadiness of your gaze, the ease or tension in your body.

Especially in moments of tension or uncertainty, people are not consciously evaluating every word or expression. Their nervous system is doing the work—scanning for safety long before their thoughts organize. On a subconscious level, questions arise before language forms: Do I feel safe here? Can I trust this person? Do I lean in—or pull away?

That instant, physiological read shapes perception more than any role, status, or carefully chosen words. Before logic engages, the body decides. That is why emotional steadiness, tone, and grounded energy matter as much as content. People do not just hear you—they feel you. And that feeling determines whether trust grows or resistance forms.

Like it or not, people experience you first through how you show up—not through your résumé, reputation, or achievements. Within seconds, they form an impression of whether you seem grounded, genuine, and emotionally intelligent. Before you speak a word, that impression is already underway.

Your presence is a living résumé, constantly updating with every micro-expression, pause, and gesture. The way you occupy space reflects your internal architecture—your emotional awareness, self-regulation, and confidence. It signals whether you can be trusted, respected, or followed.

The goal is not to look confident but to be confident—to let your internal state and external energy align. Consider a leader who navigates a tense meeting with calm, values-driven focus, or a parent who steadies a difficult moment with patience rather than force. Both convey far more authority than someone who asserts themselves with the volume turned up while feeling uncertain inside.

No credential compensates for the absence of emotional intelligence. People may respect your position, but they respond to your emotional footprint.

When how you show up communicates safety and sincerity, you become someone around whom others can exhale. And that—more than any polished list of accomplishments—is what makes you truly unforgettable.

First Impressions

Which reaction do you most often evoke before you even speak—and why? Your energy is never neutral. It either invites connection or triggers protection.

Learners, Rightness-Seekers, and Performers

Once you understand how you show up, the next question is what kind of energy you bring when you do. Whether you are leading a team, coaching a colleague, managing a household, or casually diagnosing your friends over coffee (admit it—we have all done it), you tend to show up in one of three ways.

Most people default to a familiar mode without even realizing it—a habitual way of showing up that shapes how others experience them.

The Learner

These are the brave ones—the curious minds who arrive with humility and the courage to grow. Their energy says: I do not know it all, but I am here to find out. Learners are not chasing ideal outcomes—they are practicing attentiveness and the art of showing up. They ask real questions. They welcome feedback, even when it stings. They meet discomfort with curiosity rather than defensiveness.

Learners understand that growth is not something to perform; it is a practice.

The Rightness-Seeker

Then there are the Rightness-Seekers—the "let me explain why I am right" contingent. They enter conversations as if they are making a case, often serving as both advocate and judge. Winning quietly takes priority over understanding. They tend to defend more than they listen and reassure themselves more than they reflect. Many are incredibly bright—but sometimes that brilliance turns inward and becomes blinding. In their effort to be right, they miss opportunities to be real.

The Performer

And finally, the Performers. They say the right words, nod at the right times, and can even access emotion when the moment calls for it. They appear engaged. They sound self-aware. Yet beneath that polished surface often lives quiet exhaustion—the strain of maintaining the image of "doing well." Performers frequently say, "I have tried everything," and in many ways, they genuinely believe they have. But much of their effort remains on the surface: familiar strategies repeated, deeper work postponed, and doors left unopened because what lies behind them feels uncertain or uncomfortable. Their intentions are sincere, but intention alone is not the same as engaging in true inner work.

Which Mode Leads?

*When pressure rises, which version of you shows up first—
the Learner, the Performer, or the Rightness-Seeker?
You cannot shift what you refuse to see.*

The Tie-in

This is not about shaming; it is about naming. Once you can name your pattern (or patterns), you create the possibility of choosing differently. We all move through these modes at different points in our lives. The goal is not doing this without missteps. The goal is awareness.

Notice when you are trying to impress instead of connect. When you are defending instead of reflecting. When you are performing instead of growing. And notice with whom—and under what circumstances—this tends to happen. There is wisdom in those patterns.

How you show up mentally and emotionally is just as powerful as how you show up physically. Growth cannot happen through a script. Transformation does not occur while you are performing. And leadership cannot be sustained from a place of control or concealment.

Bring the Learner—especially when it feels uncomfortable, uncertain, or vulnerable. That is where presence deepens. That is where growth becomes real. And that is where authentic leadership quietly begins.

Curiosity over Control

In your next hard conversation, ask yourself:
Am I here to understand—or to win?
The Learner leads by listening, not by proving.

Mood Matters. Always

Emotions are contagious. We are all walking, talking petri dishes of feelings, brushing past one another and spreading whatever emotional chemistry we happen to be cultivating that day. Maintaining emotional hygiene is part of showing up fully—your inner state shapes the energy you carry into every space. Whether you realize it or not, you leave an emotional fingerprint on every room you enter.

That sharp tone, that well-aimed sigh, that flash of irritation disguised as humor—it all travels faster than you think. Emotional residue lingers. People might forget your words, but they will remember how it felt to be around you.

The reverse is also true. A calm steadiness, grounded optimism, or quiet confidence that says, "We have this." can shift an entire room's emotional temperature. Humor, patience, curiosity, and genuine attentiveness have a way of softening edges, disarming tension, and inspiring trust.

The choice is yours, but the effect is real. People feel your energy long before they process your language. They calibrate to it—rising, relaxing, or retreating depending on what you bring into the space. This does not begin at the doorway. It begins within.

Before you influence anyone else, you are influencing yourself. You are in constant dialogue with your own mind—narrating, interpreting, reacting. The question is: what kind of tone does that inner conversation have?

Are you speaking to yourself with patience, honesty, and compassion—or criticizing yourself before you even have a chance to show up fully? The tone of that internal dialogue sets the baseline for every external interaction.

If your inner world is full of pressure, judgment, or self-doubt, it seeps out—through your posture, your tone, your silences, your sighs. But when your internal voice is kind, steady, and self-respecting, people feel that too.

Be generous with yourself. Encourage yourself the way you would a trusted friend. Treat yourself with the same dignity you hope others will extend to you. How you show up externally is always a reflection of how you are showing up internally.

Showing up fully does not start at the doorway—it begins in the stillness of your own mind before you ever walk into the room.

The Emotional Residue

What emotion do people carry after you leave the room—calm, tension, warmth, pressure? Your impact lingers.
Treat it with care.

Empathy, Presence, and the Quiet Power of Influence

Empathy is the ability to sense and understand another's experience while remaining fully grounded in your own presence. It is the cornerstone of your emotional footprint. It is more than feeling for others—it is feeling with them. Empathy is engagement with intention: listening deeply, responding thoughtfully, and choosing care over convenience.

Empathy in action is compassion.

And compassion is not soft or sentimental. It is strength wrapped in calm. It is discipline wrapped in grace. It is leadership in its most human form. Every interaction becomes an opportunity to listen without interruption, to hold space without judgment, and to model steadiness under pressure.

If you hold any role of influence—parent, supervisor, friend, coach, or teammate—you are leading. The question is not whether you lead; it is how.

Leadership is not about being in charge. It is about how you carry yourself when no one is watching. It is professionalism in its quietest form—integrity that does not require an audience. It is discretion with other people's stories, respect for their dignity, and reverence for their vulnerability.

True leadership understands that collaboration is not about getting your way. It is about finding the way—together.

How you show up is itself an act of leadership. It is what people feel when you are with them and what they notice when you are not. When you scroll through your phone during a conversation, reply to notifications mid-meeting, or half listen while mentally drafting your next task, you send a message. It is not subtle. It says: My attention is negotiable.

Your time, focus, and energy are finite currencies. How you spend them reveals your priorities more honestly than any mission statement ever could. Showing up fully is a form of respect—for yourself and for others. That kind of presence builds credibility and trust faster than any title or speech.

Even silence is part of your relational signal. The pauses you take, the breaths between words, the moments you choose to simply listen—all of it communicates. Silence can project confidence, patience, and reflection. It can also reveal discomfort, distraction, or disengagement. The difference lies in intention.

Mastering quiet influence means knowing when to speak, when to hold space, and when to let the moment breathe. Every glance, nod, and pause contributes to the story you are telling about who you are.

How you show up is the quiet architecture of trust. Over time, it shapes how the world experiences you. Credentials fade; influence lingers. People remember whether they felt seen, heard, and valued (or dismissed, minimized, and drained) through their encounter with you.

This is the long game: the quiet, consistent pattern of how you show up in small moments that compounds into trust, credibility, and influence.

Here is the truth: You are always communicating. Always sending a message. Opting out is not an option. The only choice you have is which signal you are sending. If you want to be experienced as credible, grounded, and deeply human, it starts here. Master the unspoken language that precedes every word you say. Your presence is your living résumé—and it follows you everywhere, whether you notice it or not.

How you show up does not end with what you say or even how you listen. It lives in the subtleties—the micro-expressions, posture shifts, and raised eyebrows you may not realize you are broadcasting. Long before you speak, your face has already told the room a story. Sometimes it is not the story you intended to tell.

When your internal state and external expression do not match— when your words say, "I'm fine," but your face communicates "Barely"—people feel the dissonance. Emotional congruence matters.

Your energy will always reveal what your script attempts to conceal.

The Quiet Seen

*When was the last time someone felt truly seen by you?
What made that moment different—your stillness, your tone,
your restraint? Your presence carries the most weight in what
you do not rush.*

Fix Your Face (Yes, We See That)

Empathy and attention are not abstract ideals—they live in the micro-moments. The pause before you respond. The tone you choose. The glance you give. The way you look at someone while they are speaking tells them everything about whether it is safe to keep going.

Which brings us to the next part of this conversation—your face.

For all the focus we place on words and tone, most people underestimate how much their expression communicates. Long before your leadership philosophy, your emotional intelligence, or your carefully chosen words register, your face has already delivered a message.

Every raised eyebrow, side-eye, slow blink, or thousand-yard stare is part of your communication toolkit. Often, those expressions speak far louder than your words ever could.

Here is the uncomfortable truth: You may think you are hiding frustration, masking boredom, or camouflaging doubt, but your face is often renting a neon billboard that reads, *"This meeting could have been an email."*

Nonverbal signals are powerful—and they are never neutral. Your silence is not silent; it is an open canvas for interpretation. And people love to interpret.

This is not about vanity, nor an invitation to "smile more." It is about nonverbal emotional intelligence: recognizing that your resting face is rarely resting. It is telling a story. If you do not take ownership of that story, others will fill in the blanks—and their version may not be generous or accurate.

Your face is constantly broadcasting information. A furrowed brow might mean concentration, not criticism. Pursed lips may signal thoughtfulness, not irritation. But unless you provide context, people will project meaning onto your expression—often filtered through their own insecurities.

This is where presence becomes either leadership gold or kryptonite. When people interpret your expression as disapproving or disengaged, they adjust. They share less. They brace more. Before you realize it, you have become hard to talk to.

It may not feel fair—but it is deeply human. People are wired to read emotional safety through nonverbal cues long before words are exchanged. In the absence of context, your face becomes the loudest voice in the room. Even in silence, others are scanning micro-expressions, posture shifts, and subtle reactions while their nervous system quietly asks: *Can I speak freely? Will I be respected? Is it safe to be honest here?*

Your expression answers those questions before your words ever do. A raised eyebrow, an eye roll, or a tightened jaw can communicate more than a paragraph of explanation. The body does not wait for language—it broadcasts your internal state in real time. That is why self-awareness is not just emotional intelligence; it is leadership in motion. The energy behind your face becomes the environment others work, speak, and breathe within.

Now, let us talk about micro-reactions. Do your eyes widen every time someone offers an idea you do not love? Do you sigh when a certain colleague starts talking? Are your shoulders permanently hovering near your ears? These small, unconscious cues create an emotional climate that whispers, *"Don't bother."*

Over time, those moments shape reputation. Words fade, but the emotional footprint you leave lingers. Not because people are fragile—because they are observant.

Your neutral is not neutral to anyone else. Brains crave predictability and resist uncertainty. When your face looks tense, people assume something is wrong. When you look skeptical, they prepare for criticism. When you look annoyed, they stop talking.

You can break that cycle with one simple practice: narrate your face. Truly. A quick, *"Ignore my expression—I am just thinking,"* or *"That is my processing face, not my judgment face,"* can shift the room instantly. It reassures people that they are safe, that your expression is not a threat, and that you are self-aware enough to name it. People do not need polished answers—they need understanding.

Nonverbal emotional intelligence is not about faking warmth; it is about aligning intention with expression. If your goal is openness, curiosity, or thoughtful engagement, your face and body need to reflect it. When intention and expression align, people feel it.

Leadership and influence are negotiated in every interaction. Your words matter, but your expressions amplify—or undercut—them. A calm, open face can turn an ordinary exchange into a moment of trust. Fix your face—not because it is wrong, but because it is powerful.

Your face is your PR manager, your brand ambassador, your emotional handshake. Make sure it is working for you, not against you. Lead with awareness. Lead with intention. You are leading whether you mean to or not—so you may as well lead on purpose.

Your expressions are the prologue that shapes how every word lands. Honor them. Guide them. Align them. When you do, people will not just hear you—they will feel safer with you, trust you more deeply, and follow your lead with less hesitation.

Your face tells the room how safe it is to be human. Those micro-moments and subtle reactions shape the emotional temperature of the space. Leadership is not just what you intend to communicate—it is what people actually experience.

And that brings us here.

Face Awareness Check

What story is your face telling right now? Is it aligned with the message you intend to send? Your face speaks first.
Make sure it is telling the truth you mean to lead with.

How Others Experience You (Hint: Ask)

Here is the uncomfortable truth: Self-awareness means little if it never leaves your own mind. You may believe you are calm, empathetic, or approachable—but that only matters if it is how people actually experience you. Bridging the gap between internal intention and external impact is where emotional intelligence meets real-world courage.

And that courage begins with one deceptively simple question: How do others experience me?

Then comes the harder part—actually asking.

Not just your supporters. Not the people who think every idea you have is exceptional. Ask the ones who have seen you impatient, distracted, or under pressure. Ask the truth-tellers. The people who care enough to be honest, not just agreeable.

Try asking:
- What is it like to be led by me?
- What is it like to work with me?
- What is it like to disagree with me?

Now pause for the internal resistance: Why should I care what other people think? Because you do not live—or lead—in isolation. Leadership, trust, and real collaboration depend on one critical alignment: your intention and their experience. When those two diverge, sincerity can land as confusion and good intentions can quietly miss their mark.

Understanding how others experience you is not about people-pleasing. It is about integrity. When your self-perception aligns with lived impact, you create resonance. When it does not, you create friction.

Not every opinion deserves a seat at your table. Seek feedback from people invested in your growth, not your comfort. Listen for patterns rather than outliers. The goal is not perfection—it is congruence between who you believe you are and how others feel in your presence. That alignment is the work—and the gift—of emotionally intelligent leadership.

Feedback is not an attack. It is a mirror.
And mirrors, when you are willing to look, help you grow.

Feedback does not need to be flattering to be constructive. It reveals how your energy, tone, and behavior land in the real world. Ignoring it does not protect you; it limits you. Courageous leaders do not avoid feedback—they metabolize it.

Once you begin looking honestly, the next question naturally follows: How do you show up once you know?

Awareness is only the first step.
Showing up fully is the practice.

Intention vs. Impact

What story are you broadcasting without realizing it—through tone, timing, or tension? Where might your intent and your impact be out of sync? People believe what they feel long before they analyze what you mean.

The Art of Showing Up

The power of undistracted, one-on-one time is simple but profound. A protected window with no phone, no multitasking, no divided attention. Just one person showing up fully for another.

Now imagine bringing that same intention into your adult relationships—your partner, your team, your colleagues. Saying, "I am here. You have my full attention." Blocking time and actually honoring it. Not pretending to listen while half-typing an email. Not glancing at your phone. Not mentally drafting your next obligation. Just genuine, undivided presence.

Call it Focus Time, Zero-Distraction Minutes, or Just-You-Time—whatever helps you commit to it. Because this level of attentiveness is not only a gift; it is a discipline. Radical, even, in a world addicted to notifications. Your full engagement communicates something no title or credential ever could:

You matter. I am here. Fully.

But showing up is not only physical. It is mental and emotional availability, too.

It means preparing before you walk in.
It means listening while you are actually there—not while thinking about dinner, deadlines, or your next rebuttal.

It means allowing the moment to have you—your steadiness, your softness, your self-awareness.

And here is the part most people miss: that same intentional availability is required for yourself.

If you never offer yourself your own full attention—time to think, decompress, reset, and breathe—how can you offer it to anyone else? Showing up for others begins with showing up for yourself.

Your presence is your résumé—your real résumé.

It enters every room before you speak. It shapes how safe people feel being honest with you, disagreeing with you, or bringing you their messy, unpolished truth. How you show up teaches others what is safe, what is expected, and what is possible.

Show up or Step Aside

When pressure rises, your energy communicates something—calm, chaos, or control. Reliability may not be glamorous, but it is unforgettable.

You do not need to solve everything instantly. You do not need the polished response. But you do need to pause. Breathe. Reset.

Thoughtfulness is not hesitation—it is leadership.

This is one of the cornerstones of showing up well: choosing intentional expression over impulsive reaction.

Reliability, consistency, preparedness, and follow-through are not corporate buzzwords; they are emotional contracts. They tell people you are steady in the storm and not someone who melts, lashes out, or transfers stress onto whoever is closest.

If you are going to show up, then show up—fully, honestly, and truly. Not to impress. Not to collect approval points. But because integrity matters more than image.

People notice what you do, but they feel how you do it.

They feel the difference between:
- Listening and waiting to speak
- Curiosity and control
- Presence and performative calm
- Grounded leadership and frantic self-protection

And the hard moments—the conflict, the uncertainty, the pressure—reveal your leadership far more than the polished ones ever will.

The Moments That Tell the Truth

How do people experience you in conflict, in change, in silence, and under pressure? These moments reveal more than any credentials ever could.

The Power of the Pause

The pause is your secret weapon. Free. Exquisite. Always available; quietly waiting for you to choose it. It is how you shift from being reactive to being intentional. That single moment of stillness before you respond is where real power lives.

To navigate tension effectively, you must first see what is actually happening beneath the surface. That requires full engagement—no autopilot, no half listening, no emotional hijacking. A pause creates space to gather information, notice subtle cues, and understand the emotions driving the moment.

One pause before responding can save a relationship, preserve trust, or protect your own dignity. One steady breath can keep a conversation from spiraling. One second of curiosity can replace defensiveness with understanding. This is not hesitation or weakness—it is skill. The pause is the heartbeat of de-escalation, and de-escalation is the cornerstone of effective leadership.

Remember this: Never outsource your self-worth to others. If someone fails to see your value, that is their blind spot—not yours. How you show up matters. Your energy is felt. Own it. Use the pause to lead with compassion, steadiness, and emotional intelligence.

***

The Power of One Breath

When was the last time you paused before reacting?
Every breath between impulse and response is an opportunity to
choose peace over ego, steadiness over chaos.

***

No More Shrinking

I cannot say this enough: If your values are clear and aligned, stand firmly in them. Stand with courage, conviction, and respect. That does not mean bulldozing others—but it does mean refusing to dim your light to keep others comfortable. Every time you shrink yourself, you trade authenticity for approval—and that trade never ends well.

The sense of worth you have cultivated becomes the foundation for how you show up—your anchor when choosing not to shrink. Worth is the quiet conviction that you belong exactly as you are. Presence is how that conviction moves through the world.

Every interaction is an opportunity to live your values out loud—to model the kind of humanity you want to see more of. People are always watching, but more importantly, they are always feeling. They feel your steadiness. Your tone. Your energy. Energy is contagious. Whether you intend it or not, you become a living example of what you stand for.

Grand gestures are not required to make an impact. One calm tone instead of a snap. One clear correction instead of silence. One kind word instead of criticism. Small moments shift entire dynamics. You may never see the full ripple of your courage—but it matters. Your refusal to shrink is a gift to yourself and to everyone around you.

The Ripple You Created

*Recall one recent moment when you chose calm over fear
or honesty over avoidance. That was not small—it was proof that
your alignment speaks louder than fear.*

Own the Room You Walk Into

Owning the room is not about dominating it. It is about honoring it. It is not about being the loudest voice or having the most polished presence. It is about sensing what the space needs and meeting it with confidence, humility, and intention—without losing yourself.

Be steady. Be kind. Be curious. Be human. Those qualities will do more for your credibility and influence than any title ever could.

Show up on purpose. Show up as if you mean it. Fix your face. Soften your voice. Breathe before speaking. Pause before reacting. Read the energy before adding to it. Your stillness sets the tone. Your self-awareness becomes the anchor.

This is presence.
This is emotional intelligence.
This is leadership.
This is humanity at its best.

No more shrinking.
No more performing.
No more halfway.

If you are going to show up, show up all the way. Let your steadiness speak louder than fear. Let groundedness lead louder than ego. The room does not need you to be polished—it needs you to be real.

How you show up is not merely your style—it is your signal. It teaches people how to treat you, how to trust you, and how to value you.

It shows them what safety feels like, what calm leadership looks like, and what integrity sounds like in motion.

None of this works unless you believe you are worth showing up for. Showing up without self-worth becomes performance. But when worth and presence align, you become the steady pulse others calibrate to—the grounded energy that steadies chaos and invites real connection.

Owning the Room

When you walk into a space, what arrives with you—calm or chaos? The energy you bring teaches others how to meet you, trust you, and follow your lead. Arrive as if you already belong.

Your Presence Speaks — Then Your Words Finish the Sentence

Presence is how you enter the room.
Words are what you leave behind.

Every sentence you speak carries weight. Every yes, every no, every offhand comment leaves an imprint—on trust, on relationships, on credibility. Words are not merely tools; they are declarations. They reveal your values, your emotional maturity, and your sense of self-worth.

It is one thing to show up fully. It is another to speak with intention, integrity, and credibility—to choose language that aligns with who you are and what you stand for. The words you choose become your emotional signature. They can build trust, inspire action, and calm storms—or quietly unravel everything you have worked to establish.

Your words carry emotional weight even when you do not intend them to. A sigh, a sharp tone, a careless remark travels faster than intention. Yet when language is chosen consciously, it can steady a team, repair tension, or restore energy to exhausted spaces.

Make no mistake: words are energy. They shape the emotional climate around you. They can ground a conversation or ignite conflict. They can signal safety or broadcast judgment.

If presence is the stage, language is the performance—and it matters. The next step is learning to speak with the same calm integrity you carry, using words that are clear, deliberate, and grounded in truth. People may first experience how you show up, but they will remember what you say.

The Bridge to Words

The Echo of Integrity

Do your words reflect the same steadiness and integrity as the way you show up? If presence sets the tone, language defines the story. Speak as if your words will echo in someone's mind long after you leave the room—because they will.

Language as Leadership

What tone follows you when you leave a conversation—calm or chaos? Every word carries energy. Let yours model composure, care, and clarity. People remember how you made them feel more than what you said.

The Weight of Your Voice

When emotion rises, can your words still align with your values? Pause before you speak. The language you choose in moments of tension reveals your truest leadership—and your truest self.

Chapter 8:
Words Matter, "Dammit!!"

All of this—presence, pause, consistency, authenticity—sets the stage. Showing up fully, with intention, self-awareness, and integrity matters. But being in the room is only part of the equation. Once you have earned trust and attention, the next step is just as critical: the words you choose. Presence opens the door; words determine whether people stay, trust, and take you seriously. That is where we turn next.

What Comes Out of Your Mouth Has Power

We spend so much time worrying about what not to say—the traps, triggers, and careless remarks that spark conflict or quietly corrode trust. Yes, restraint is part of emotional intelligence. But the other side is just as powerful: the intentional use of words that strengthen relationships, restore trust, and make someone feel genuinely seen and safe around you. Those sentences are rarely accidental. They are chosen.

Words are never without consequence. They are bridges, anchors, and mirrors. They shape the emotional climate of every conversation and every room—because people assign meaning based on past experiences, identity, and context (Blumer, 1986). Used with care, words become the foundation of respect and belonging. Used carelessly, they can fracture trust in a single breath.

Every agreement, refusal, or offhand comment sends a signal. You are always broadcasting meaning, whether you realize it or not.

Words give shape to your emotional signature. Unlike the energy you radiate—which people absorb unconsciously—words offer a blueprint others use to understand who you are, what you value, and how seriously to take you.

When words build rather than break, everything changes. A staff member came into a meeting visibly tense, bracing for blame. Instead, their director said, *"You are not in trouble. I want to understand what happened so we can solve it together."* The atmosphere shifted instantly. Shoulders dropped. Defensiveness dissolved. One thoughtful sentence opened the door to accountability without shame.

When words break instead of build, the impact is just as immediate. Contrast that scenario with a leader who begins with: *"Explain what you messed up this time."* No facts have been exchanged, yet psychological safety has already been shattered. One sentence undermines trust, inflames ego, and signals how mistakes will be handled going forward. And because negative language carries a heavier emotional impact than positive language, the damage lingers far beyond the moment.

Owning the power of your words means recognizing their capacity to clarify confusion, create calm where tension lives, and call forth truth where silence has settled. Words can open space—or shrink it. They can repair—or rupture. And even silence carries a message; how you use it determines what others hear beneath the surface.

Presence may get you into the room. Your words determine whether people stay, trust, follow, and believe. Consider how often your language repairs what ego once damaged.

Wordsmith or Wrecking Ball?

When was the last time your words built a bridge instead of a wall? Language either repairs what ego damages—or deepens the divide.

Words as Fingerprints of Your Values

Your words do not exist in a vacuum. They are fingerprints of your values, leaving impressions everywhere you go. Every phrase, tone, and choice carries evidence of what matters to you. How you communicate is inseparable from how you perceive yourself—and how you regard others.

When your language aligns with your values, people do not just hear it, they sense it. That congruence builds trust, softens defensiveness, and invites collaboration. Alignment between speech and principal signals steadiness and integrity without needing to be announced. Consistency becomes credibility (Johnston, McKee, & Boyatzis, 2008).

When your words drift from your values, credibility does not collapse dramatically—it unravels quietly. You speak of shared ownership but assign blame when things go sideways. You emphasize respect but interrupt without noticing. Integrity rarely fractures through grand betrayals; it erodes through subtle contradictions.

The Communication Gap

A manager says, *"My door is always open,"* yet rushes through check-ins, rarely truly listens, and shows irritation at interruptions. There is no malice—just mixed signals. Before long, staff stop bringing concerns forward. Not because of the words themselves, but because the behavior behind them did not match the promise.

Availability cannot be declared; it has to be felt. When words suggest openness but behavior communicates strain, people trust behavior. Language loses credibility. Over time, communication does not break—it withdraws.

The alignment gap is rarely loud. It shows up in fewer questions, shorter conversations, and carefully edited honesty. And by the time leaders notice the quiet, trust has already shifted.

The Echo Check

When today did your words reflect your principles—and when did they slip into habit, hurry, or heat? Awareness begins in the space between the two.

Compliments That Land

Let us start with the constructive side: compliments. Not the hollow, automatic *"nice job"* variety—the kind that makes people feel genuinely seen and supported. Real compliments are not throwaway niceties; they are emotional structure. They shape the atmosphere of a team, a partnership, a family, a room.

Psychologists have long observed that affirmations create belonging in ways criticism never can (Baumeister et al., 2001). Consider what happens when you tell a colleague, *"I feel like you hear me even when I am struggling to explain something."* That is not mere praise; that is reassurance. Or when you tell a friend, *"You make space for whichever version of me shows up,"* you are naming emotional refuge. These are not decorative words. They are grounding.

Thoughtful affirmation strengthens connection on both sides. It trains the speaker to notice what is true and worthwhile and gives the listener a mirror that reflects their value back to them. This is not flattery. It is attunement.

When a compliment is specific and sincere, it becomes a deposit in the emotional bank account of trust. Unlike financial accounts, the return grows the more you contribute.

A Moment of Recognition

Sometimes the smallest phrases steady a relationship and restore perspective:
I know this is a lot. Thank you for sticking with it.
You stepped up today, and it mattered.
You helped more than you realize.

These statements are not simply positive feedback; they recalibrate the relational dynamic. They acknowledge effort, intention, and resilience. They signal that trust remains intact, even in stressful circumstances.

Each line validates and anchors the relationship in honesty. It reminds the other person that something essential is still working. Recognition clarifies the emotional temperature of a moment, and often, it defuses anxiety before it forms.

Recognition as Restoration

When was the last time you acknowledged someone's steadiness, integrity, or courage? Recognition is not flattery. It is feedback that restores trust and reinforces belonging.

Names: The Simplest Words with the Deepest Weight

A name is never just a label. It is identity, memory, belonging, and the first signal of respect. When you remember and use someone's name, you are communicating "I see you. I value you. You matter enough for me to pay attention." Calling someone by name is one of the simplest interpersonal signals of dignity and belonging.

In a classroom, a professor who learns dozens of names in the first few weeks is not merely performing a task. They are communicating safety, welcome, and intentional inclusion. That level of effort transforms the room. It raises the standard. Why do we reserve that level of attention for only certain environments?

Now consider the opposite: someone repeatedly mispronounces your name, shortens it without permission, or forgets it entirely. It does not feel small. It feels erasing. It signals indifference, even when unintentional. The underlying message becomes: You are not significant enough to remember. And that message settles far deeper than most realize.

Leaders who know and use people's names build trust more quickly. Teachers who learn their students' names strengthen the psychological safety of the room. Everyday exchanges—in the hallway, in a meeting, on a Zoom call—become moments of genuine connection when someone is addressed by name. It costs nothing yet carries profound weight.

Names carry history. They carry culture. They carry meaning. Learning to pronounce someone's name correctly is not simply polite—it is an act of honoring who they are. And if you mispronounce it, own it. Apologize. Practice until you get it right. That effort speaks volumes about respect, intentionality, and emotional intelligence.

So, if words matter—and they absolutely do—then names matter most of all. They are the bridge between just another person and a human being you are choosing to see. Using them is not just courtesy. It is leadership. It is emotional intelligence. It is respect.

Names Are Not Small

How does it feel when someone remembers your name versus when they do not? Small moments of attention reveal the depth of how we show up.

Micro-Miracles in Everyday Language

Not all impact comes from speeches or dramatic declarations. Some of the most transformative words are the simplest—precisely because we attach shared meaning to them beyond the syllables themselves.

Thank you.
    I see you.
        You matter.

These are micro-miracles: tiny moments of recognition that strengthen relationships thread by thread. A sincere compliment. A pause to listen without rushing. A brief acknowledgment of effort. These gestures cost nothing, yet they reinforce meaning in ways that linger quietly beneath the surface.

One sentence can change an entire emotional climate. Saying to a teammate, *"I noticed how calmly you handled that situation,"* does more than express appreciation—it communicates steadiness, confidence, and trust. Simple words, placed intentionally, can anchor someone battling uncertainty.

Micro-miracles are the small relational deposits that compound into loyalty, stability, and shared respect. Their power is symbolic, not theatrical. The smallest words often carry the deepest impact because they affirm belonging without spectacle.

The research is clear: Brief moments of verbal affirmation activate the same reward pathways associated with safety, bonding, and emotional security.

The beauty is you do not need authority, title, or permission to offer them. Only attention, intention, and courage.

Words That Stay

When was the last time your words helped someone feel support-ed, respected, or steadied? Even the smallest acknowledgment can quietly redirect an entire moment.

The Other Side of the Mouth

Every word carries energy. Some repair; some rupture. Words can corrode trust in a single flat moment. They can undermine relationships, fracture teams, and leave scars that far outlast the conversation that caused them.

Words are currency. Each phrase either builds a connection or slowly deteriorates it. And here is a truth many resist: more words do not mean more understanding. If your language is unfiltered, defensive, gossipy, or laced with hostile sarcasm, you are not communicating—you are causing harm.

Communication is only as strong as the transparency, intention, and alignment behind it. If you are not clear on what you are saying or why you are saying it, do not expect to be understood. People feel the meaning beneath words long before they analyze the words themselves.

Every sentence sends a signal about who you are and the kind of space you create. Over time, your language teaches others how safe it is to approach you, how honest they can be with you, and whether you can be trusted with vulnerability.

Words can heal, guide, and anchor—or they can erode, confuse, and divide. The choice is always present. Speak with awareness. Speak with purpose. Speak in alignment with your values.

Once words are spoken, there is no rewind—only the echoes that follow.

Word Choice and Microaggressions

When your words do not match your actions, people do not hear your intentions—they experience contradiction. Consistency matters. A hollow *I care about you* means nothing if it is followed by disregard. Words without alignment are not leadership—they are theater.

It helps to name the ways language can harm—because the damage is rarely dramatic. It is usually quiet.

Misalignment is when language promises support, care, or stability, but behavior contradicts it. A leader says, *"Your well-being matters,"* then repeatedly schedules late-night deadlines. A friend says, *"You can always be honest with me,"* then reacts defensively the moment honesty arrives. A manager says, *"We are a team,"* then publicly singles out individuals when things go wrong. The words sound safe. The experience is not.

Sarcasm can build closeness when it is rooted in trust. But when it is used to avoid discomfort or dodge accountability, it cuts instead of connects. Someone opens up, and the response is, *"Wow, sounds like you are really crushing it,"* drenched in irony. A colleague shares a mistake and hears, *"Great—just what we needed,"* with a smirk. There may be laughter, but there is also distance.

And then there are **microaggressions**—subtle stings that communicate dismissal, minimization, or othering through tone, phrasing, emphasis, or expression. *You are being too sensitive. Calm down—it's not that serious. Are you sure you can handle this? It's complicated.* Delivered with doubt, not care. Individually, they seem small. Collectively, they erode belonging.

Here is the difficult truth: intent does not cancel impact. Even when harm was unintentional, the effect still lands. Emotional intelligence requires awareness of that gap—and accountability for the environments we shape, whether we mean to or not.

A Moment of Empathy

Recall a time when someone's words or tone made you feel dismissed or unseen. What shifted inside you? Let that memory guide how you speak when it matters.

The Lens Problem: Said, Heard, Meant

Here is where communication becomes complicated: every person filters words through their own lens—shaped by culture, upbringing, past experiences, and environment. In plain terms, we respond not to the words themselves but to the meaning we assign them.

Which means: What you said is not always what was heard. What was heard is not always what you meant.

That gap is fertile ground for misunderstanding. It explains why someone storms away angry while you are left confused. It is why relationships fracture over "just words," why emails ignite conflict that was never intended, and why feedback sometimes lands like a punch instead of a bridge. And thanks to the brain's negativity bias, negative interpretations often carry more weight than neutral or positive ones (Baumeister et al., 2001).

The fix is deceptively simple—and deceptively hard:
Listen to understand, not to respond.
Check assumptions before reacting.
Slow down when emotions rise.

Clarifying intentions before speaking is not optional; it is foundational.

One Email, Three Interpretations

Meeting Version
You say in a meeting: Let's circle back later.
You mean: We need more information first.
They hear: Your idea is not worth discussing.
You intended direction.
They heard dismissal.

Leadership / HR Setting
You offer a colleague: This could be stronger with a few adjustments.
You mean: You are close—just polish it.
They hear: This is not good enough.
You intended support.
They heard criticism.

Personal Relationship Setting
You text: We need to talk.
You mean: Let's connect later.
They hear: Something is wrong.
You intended coordination.
They heard panic.

One sentence… three different emotional realities.

Here is a practical rule: do not send the email, start the feedback, or begin the conversation when your emotional thermostat is overheated. A pause is not avoidance—it is protection. It safeguards your integrity, your relationships, and the trust you are trying to preserve. One moment of patience can prevent weeks—or years—of misunderstanding.

Think of communication as a bridge, not a weapon. The stronger the bridge, the safer the crossing. And that bridge is built one careful, intentional word at a time.

When Impact Surprised You

*When did a casual comment land differently than you intended?
What did that moment reveal about perspective—
yours and theirs?*

The Discipline of Speaking Less and Saying More

One of the most undervalued life and leadership skills is discernment: knowing when to contribute and when to listen. Words are powerful, but restraint is a superpower. Speaking without intention dilutes impact, invites misinterpretation, and broadcasts unprocessed emotion. Every unnecessary word increases the risk of missing the mark.

Discipline in speech is not silence for its own sake. It is precision. It is care. It is choosing to respond over impulse. It asks you to pause long enough to consider: Does this add value? Does this clarify? Does this honor trust? Or am I filling space, defending ego, or reacting from a trigger?

Speaking less forces your words to matter. A measured sentence lands with weight; a flood of unfiltered commentary lands as noise. Research shows that meaning and interpretation—not volume—are what shape how words are received. A single intentional sentence can anchor a room, while fifty careless ones scatter focus and confidence everywhere. Impact is not about quantity—it is about accuracy.

Restraint is not weakness. It is strength under control. It is one of the highest forms of self-respect and emotional maturity. Not every thought deserves a stage. Not every emotion requires a microphone. Not every opinion needs an audience.

It takes real discipline to recognize the moment silence carries more weight than speech. When anger rises—pause. When gossip tempts—pause. When sarcasm lines up at the door—pause. Those small pauses are acts of leadership. They protect your integrity and the dignity of others.

Restraint does more than prevent harm—it preserves relational balance. It protects trust. It keeps relationships intact. It prevents the kind of wounds that take years to heal. Silence, used wisely, signals steadiness and self-command. It gives others space to think, breathe, and join you without fear.

Restraint does not mean withholding honesty. It means delivering honesty responsibly. Louder volume is not clarity. Impulse is not leadership. And cruelty disguised as just being honest is still cruelty.

The skill is choosing the right words, at the right time, for the right reasons.

Your silence can be your credibility.
Your pause can be your protection.
Your restraint can be your greatest source of influence.

The Impulse Tax

Where have your quick reactions created unnecessary tension?
Your first reaction is instinct. Your chosen response is character.

Handling Difficult Conversations with Intentional Language

Difficult conversations are unavoidable. Whether you are addressing underperformance, confronting conflict, or setting expectations, the words you choose can either escalate tension or build understanding.

Intentional language transforms these moments from emotional minefields into opportunities for clarity, growth, and strengthened trust.

Start with intention. Know exactly what you want to communicate and why. Ambiguity is the enemy of understanding. Before you speak, ask yourself: *What is my purpose here? What outcome am I aiming for? How does this reflect the respect I owe the other person?* Precision of intention is the foundation of effective communication—especially when the stakes are high (Johnston, McKee, & Boyatzis, 2008).

Lead with empathy. Difficult conversations are rarely only about facts; they are about feelings. Acknowledge the other person's experience without weakening your message. Simple phrases, such as *"I understand this has been challenging,"* or *"I hear how this feels,"* communicate respect, reduce defensiveness, and open space for dialogue rather than debate. Research consistently shows that empathy increases psychological safety and improves cooperation in conflict settings (Greene, 2016).

Be direct, but use care. Avoid sugarcoating that obscures your message or bluntness that wounds unnecessarily. Speak to the issue, not the person. Use *I* statements that own your perspective (*I noticed... I feel... I need...*) rather than *"You always"* or *"You never"*, which trigger resistance and shut down conversation.

Pause strategically. Silence is one of the most underused tools in difficult conversations. A well-timed pause communicates steadiness, allows reflection, and diffuses emotional intensity. It signals that you are listening, not reacting. These moments of restraint give the nervous system time to settle and prevent escalation.

Finally, close with clarity. Difficult conversations are not about venting; they are about resolution. Confirm shared understanding, clarify agreements, and outline next steps. This turns intention into forward motion and aligns what is said with what will happen next.

When you approach difficult conversations with thoughtfulness, curiosity, and empathy, they stop being obligations and become opportunities for alignment, trust, and growth. Your language becomes a tool of influence rather than harm, revealing not only what you communicate but who you are.

Reframe Before Repair

Which phrases from past conversations may have unintentionally triggered defensiveness? Tone can restore relational balance—or quietly intensify resistance.

Practical Upgrade in Real Conversations

When Your Email Has More Tone Than Content

The unfiltered instinct:
You need to stop sending toned emails.
The emotionally intelligent upgrade:
I want to talk about the tone in some recent emails. I can sense there may be frustration behind them, and I want to understand what is contributing to that and how we can constructively address concerns.

When Missing Meetings Becomes a Meeting Topic

The unfiltered instinct:
Why are you not showing up to our meetings lately?
The emotionally intelligent upgrade:
I would like to address the meetings you have missed recently. I know there may be challenges happening, and I want to understand what is getting in the way and what support you may need so we can stay aligned going forward.

When a Text Accidentally Creates Panic

The unfiltered instinct:
Hey—can we talk?
The emotionally intelligent upgrade:
When you have a minute later, I would like to connect about a couple of things. No urgency—I just want to touch base.

Delivering Bad News Without Causing More Damage

At some point, you will have to deliver bad news. No one enjoys it, but avoiding it, cushioning it, or tiptoeing around the truth almost always makes things worse. People can handle hard news. What breaks trust is disrespect, dismissal, or being blindsided. Research consistently shows that negative experiences carry a disproportionately strong psychological and emotional impact compared to positive ones—which is exactly why how you deliver difficult information matters as much as what you say.

Here is the truth many avoid: there is always a way to be both direct and kind.

Direct means you do not bury the message or disguise the truth in fluff. Kind means you deliver it with empathy and respect, preserving the other person's dignity.

Direct without kindness is brutal.
Kindness without directness is dishonest.
Together, they create clarity wrapped in respect.

Delivering bad news well requires steadiness, not speed. It means being clear and concise while still acknowledging emotional impact. It means grounding the message in shared goals and offering a constructive path forward rather than leaving someone stranded in uncertainty. And it means staying present after the words land—resisting the urge to retreat, overexplain, or disappear once discomfort peaks.

What undermines trust is not the message itself but the way it is handled. Burying truth under qualifiers, hiding behind policy, or rushing through the moment to escape your own discomfort leaves people feeling dismissed and disoriented. Avoidance does not soften the blow—it prolongs it. Half-truths do not protect—they confuse and erode trust.

When you approach hard conversations with directness grounded in compassion, something important happens. People trust you more.

They know you will not retreat when things are uncomfortable. They learn that your words can be relied on—not only when it is easy, but especially when it is difficult.

This is emotional intelligence in action.

The messenger matters as much as the message.

The Weight of Delivery

Think of a time you received difficult news. What made it land with care—or with a sting? Delivery determines whether truth heals or harms.

Praise in Public, Correct in Private

Words do not merely describe reality—they shape it. How you choose to speak about people, and where you choose to do it, sets the tone for everyone watching. This principle applies not only at work but at home, in friendships, and in everyday interactions. Context matters everywhere.

Here is a simple principle: Celebrate people out loud, correct them behind closed doors.

Public praise uplifts, motivates, and reinforces behaviors you want to see more of. Behavioral research has shown that positive reinforcement is one of the most powerful drivers of sustained behavioral change. In the workplace, acknowledging a colleague's contribution in a meeting sets a tone of respect and appreciation. At home, saying, "I really admire how you handled that," in front of your children or family members does more than honor the person—it teaches others what good looks like.

Public correction, by contrast, humiliates. It erodes trust. Social-psychological studies show that public embarrassment activates the same neural threat responses associated with physical danger. The sting lingers long after the moment ends. Private correction preserves respect. It allows honesty without spectacle. It provides accountability without humiliation. That is where real connection and growth can happen.

There are exceptions, of course: moments of public safety, urgent intervention, or institutional accountability where silence would enable harm. In those instances, stepping in publicly protects people—not pride. But even then, dignity remains the objective.

For everything else, the dirty laundry rule applies: mistakes, missteps, or interpersonal conflicts rarely belong on public display. Transparency has boundaries. Mature cultures—corporate or domestic—resolve issues with discretion, care, and humanity.

Put simply: Praise publicly. Correct privately. Handle messes within the walls where trust can be protected. This is not etiquette—it is legacy. The way you wield words in these moments shapes the climate everyone else must live in.

Communication Beyond Words

Communication is never just about what you say. Long before words register, people read your tone, posture, pacing, and emotional state. They sense whether you are grounded or reactive, open or guarded—and that perception shapes how your message lands.

Before speaking, pause and check in with yourself. Are you calm or charged? Clear or defensive? Speaking to connect or to control? When your internal state aligns with your intention, communication becomes steadier, clearer, and more human.

Every conversation carries two messages: the literal words and the emotional current beneath them. Tone signals safety or threat. Pace signals confidence or anxiety. Silence communicates too. These signals influence not only how others interpret your words, but whether they feel comfortable responding honestly.

When you become aware of these silent elements, you do not just communicate—you shape the emotional experience of the conversation.

The Final Filter: Kind, True, Necessary

By now, one truth ought to be unmistakable: Words carry weight far beyond the moment you speak them. A careless phrase can linger. A sarcastic jab can wound more deeply than intended. A truth delivered without care can fracture a relationship. The impact of your words is real—and that is precisely why a final filter matters.

The challenge is rarely knowing what to say. The challenge is choosing whether it needs to be said at all. Restraint is not silence; it is maturity. It is recognizing where your words could harm and consciously deciding not to inflict that harm. You do not have to correct every misstep or respond to every slight. Not everything requires your voice.

Honesty is not a license for cruelty. Just because something is true does not mean it belongs in the room. Your words are meant to serve, not sabotage. The filter is simple, yet profound:

Is it kind?
Is it true?
Is it necessary?

If you cannot answer yes to at least two—pause.

This is not censorship; it is intentionality. It is the difference between lobbing grenades and laying bricks. Words chosen with care build trust, respect, and credibility. Words tossed carelessly chip away at all three—and, over time, these small fractures accumulate into lasting disconnection.

Every sentence you speak is an opportunity to strengthen your connections, clarify expectations, and align your voice with your values. When you combine restraint, empathy, integrity, and presence, your influence deepens—not because you speak more but because you speak with purpose.

Disciplined communication culminates here:

Speak less.
Listen more.
Filter wisely.
Show up fully.

Influence is not measured by volume but by resonance—by how faithfully your words reflect the person you are becoming.

Guard Your Goodness

If you genuinely cannot understand why some people go out of their way to cause harm, disrupt, or diminish others, consider that confusion a blessing. It means your empathy is still intact. Protect that goodness fiercely—do not let the world harden you. One of the most powerful ways to guard it is by guarding your words.

Words reflect character. Gossip, cruelty, and dismissive remarks reveal far more about the speaker than the target. Research shows that negative language and interactions can carry disproportionate emotional weight—leaving deeper and longer-lasting psychological effects than positive ones. Words meant to cut others down often undermine your own credibility. Staying above the belt is not naïvety—it is mastery. It is self-respect. It is respect for the people around you.

Words matter. Deeply. They can wound or heal, isolate or connect, erode or build trust. They can act as microaggressions—or micro-miracles. Every decision—what you say, how you say it, and when you choose silence—is an act of emotional intelligence and leadership.

Your words outlive the moment. The micro-miracles you create ripple outward, influencing relationships, the spaces you inhabit, and trust in ways you may never witness directly.

Words matter.
More than you think.
More than you feel.
More than you intend.

Words matter.
Dammit.

The Weight of Your Words

The Integrity Filter

Before you speak, pause and ask: Do these words build or bruise? If they were echoed back to you later, would they reflect the person you intend to be?

The Echo Test

What tone follows you when you leave a conversation—calm, clarity, tension, or doubt? Your words outlive the moment. Speak as if their echo will matter—because it will.

Guarding Your Goodness

Where have you felt tempted to trade kindness for cleverness, or honesty for sharpness? Protect the part of you that still believes words can heal. That restraint is not weakness—it is leadership.

Chapter 9:
Emotional Control Is a Superpower

"You cannot control the behavior of others, but you can control your response."

– Epictetus

Emotional Control Is a Superpower

Words matter. But what you bring into the room matters even more. How you show up is power.

Emotional control is not repression. It is awareness, leverage, and leadership in real time. At the end of the day, what comes out of your mouth is not just communication—it is reputation. It is your values made audible. Every sentence is a signal. It tells people who you are, what you stand for, and whether they are safe with you.

Speak life, not noise. Compliment to connect, not to flatter. Hold your tongue when your ego wants to roar. And when you do speak, let your words be fingerprints worth leaving behind.

But words are only part of the equation. The energy behind them—your tone, posture, pace, and steadiness—determines how they land. Presence becomes the frame through which every word is interpreted. Even silence speaks.

If you have ever wondered why certain conflicts repeat themselves, why some conversations derail instantly, or why people instinctively trust you—or pull back—the answer is rarely vocabulary alone. It is the emotional climate you carry.

This is the deeper layer of emotional intelligence, moving from communication into lived expression. When inner chaos leaks out through tone, impatience, or posture, it becomes everyone's burden. You may believe you are hiding frustration or masking doubt, but your body broadcasts what your mind denies. In leadership, in love, in life—those unspoken cues matter as much as words themselves.

Emotional control is not about suppression. It is about owning your power—the kind of calm that steadies the room; the groundedness that turns noise into clarity; the restraint that protects relationships, sharpens judgment, and amplifies influence.

Welcome to the space where calm becomes your superpower—where inner stillness guides every word, every action, every decision. This is presence in motion. This is the next frontier of influence.

The Calmness That Brings Wisdom

Emotional control is not emotional shutdown. It is not pretending you feel nothing or forcing composure while quietly unraveling inside. It is not detachment.

Emotional control—also known as emotional regulation—is the ability to feel fully without letting those feelings take the wheel. It is noticing the storm without *becoming* the storm.

You see it in the leader who absorbs bad news without panicking, holds steady when others freeze, and responds with intention instead of chaos. One person's composure can reset the emotional tone of an entire room.

Master this, and you unlock one of the rarest forms of power: the ability to choose how you show up, regardless of pressure, provocation, or circumstance.

This is difficult work. Instinct tells us to react: Someone cuts us off and anger flares. A colleague dismisses our idea and defensiveness rises. A child presses every button and frustration surges. Much of this happens automatically, before awareness has a chance to intervene.

Here is the critical truth: There is a gap between stimulus and response. Most people never learn to see it. Emotional control widens that gap. And in that space, choice is born.

With practice, life stops being a chain of reactions and becomes a deliberate sequence of responses grounded in values rather than impulse. You stop giving your power away. You become someone others trust—because your steadiness creates clarity, safety, and order.

And in that calm, wisdom has room to rise—not because emotion disappears, but because emotion is guided, not governing.

The Power of the Gap

What happens in the space between your trigger and your response? Notice that brief tightening before you react. That pause is not emptiness—it is choice. It is where awareness becomes wisdom.

Respond > React

Reacting is reflexive, emotional, and impulsive. It is the nervous system's knee-jerk response—fast, loud, and often regrettable. Someone makes a cutting remark and your body interprets it as a threat, so you strike back. Someone ignores your text and your mind writes a rejection narrative in thirty seconds.

Reacting is ego-driven. It craves the microphone. It seeks validation *now*.

Responding is intentional. It is grounded and values-led. It steps back, breathes, and asks what matters most before acting. Responding does not deny feelings—it channels them.

Reacting says: *I feel attacked; I will attack back.*
Responding says: *This matters; I will handle it in a way I can stand behind later.*

Reacting escalates. Responding stabilizes. Calmness is not passivity—it is strategy. Emotional storms pass, and when they do, perspective returns. Decisions made in anger often create regret. Decisions made from steadiness preserve dignity, resolve conflict, and reinforce boundaries without destruction.

You do not need to show up the same way in every room. That is not inauthentic—it is emotionally intelligent. Read the room. Adjust delivery, not integrity. Responding without overreacting is not a one-time choice; it is a habit you strengthen with every challenging moment.

This is how impulse becomes intention—and intention becomes influence.

Impulse or Intention

When was the last time you felt the urge to react—and chose to respond instead? That single breath between impulse and action is where values take the lead.

Never Issue Consequences in the Moment

There is a simple discipline that protects both relationships and reputations: **Never issue consequences in the heat of the moment.**

When emotions are loud, ego is activated, and adrenaline is driving the bus, wisdom quietly slips out the back door. Acting while emotionally flooded feels decisive in the moment—but it almost always costs more than you intend. It is the leadership equivalent of sending an email in all caps: you may get attention, but you will not get respect.

Parents recognize this instinctively. A child pushes every button and suddenly lifelong grounding is on the table. Leaders do it too. An employee makes a mistake and, before curiosity can intervene, frustration speaks. In the moment, it feels powerful. Later, it feels reckless.

Here is the neurological truth in plain language: When you are triggered, the emotional part of your brain hijacks the reasoning part. Perspective narrows. Foresight disappears. Even thoughtful, emotionally intelligent people can say or do damaging things—not because they lack judgment but because they temporarily lose access to it.

That is why the rule matters:
When you are activated—angry, hurt, embarrassed, overwhelmed—do not decide, punish, threaten, or declare anything irreversible.

Pause.
Breathe.
Step away if needed.

Let your nervous system settle before you speak for your authority.

Real power is not in dropping the hammer.
Real power is in restraint.

Anyone can react loudly.
Few can respond wisely.

Consequences delivered with calm, clarity, and intention land deeper, last longer, and preserve dignity. They teach rather than shame. They correct without humiliating. They protect the relationship while addressing the behavior.

The pause is not weakness. It is leadership.

Reaction Has a Cost

*When did you last react before thinking—and what did it cost
you? Restraint is not silence. It is respect for your
values and the moment itself.*

Keeping Your Emotional Power Without Going Cold

Here is a common misstep: confusing emotional control with emotional distance.

You have likely worked with—or lived with—someone who prides themselves on being "unaffected." Flat tone. Unreadable expression. Minimal reaction. They believe they are demonstrating composure. In reality, they are broadcasting disconnection.

Emotional control is not emotional shutdown.

It is not bottling everything up.
It is not pretending you do not care.
It is not withdrawing behind professionalism as armor.

That is repression, not regulation.

True emotional control is warmth with boundaries. It is the ability to feel deeply without drowning. To remain empathetic without absorbing everyone else's emotional weather. To stay grounded without becoming distant or inaccessible.

You can validate someone's feelings without agreeing with them.
You can acknowledge emotion without surrendering your center.
You can be composed without being cold.

Being grounded does not mean being unavailable.
It means holding your center while staying human.

When calm turns into withdrawal, people do not feel safe—they feel shut out. And when people feel shut out, they stop being honest. They stop bringing concerns forward. They stop trusting what is happening beneath the surface.

Emotional power invites connection.
It does not freeze it out.

The Practice of Emotional Control

Emotional control matters because it shapes everything: your credibility, your relationships, your decisions, and the emotional climate you create wherever you go.

Here is the metaphor that matters:
Emotions can ride the bus—but they do not get to drive it.

Anger, fear, joy, sadness—they are all passengers. Some are loud. Some are persistent. Some try to grab the wheel. But you are the driver. You decide who gets acknowledged, who gets heard, and where you are going.

Emotions are not the enemy. They are messengers.

Anger often signals a crossed boundary.
Fear may flag risk or uncertainty.
Sadness highlights what matters most.

They provide information. They do not run the operation.

Owning your emotions means you do not dump them on everyone around you. Venting may feel relieving in the moment, but it often deepens emotional loops and creates collateral damage. Emotional control means processing feelings responsibly so that when you show up, you show up grounded.

This is stewardship, not suppression.

Practical discipline includes:
- **Naming emotions precisely** — specificity creates distance
- **Reframing perspective** — difficult is not catastrophic
- **Accepting discomfort** — emotion is information, not failure
- **Using grounding tools** — breath, movement, silence, water, reflection
- **Practicing the pause** — where instinct becomes choice

This is how emotional discipline is built: not through theory but repetition. Each pause strengthens the muscle. Each intentional response reinforces your authority over your own inner state.

You do not become unshakable by avoiding emotion.
You become unshakable by learning how to carry it.

The Space Between

Recall a recent moment you caught yourself mid-reaction. That gap was not hesitation. It was progress.

Positive Thinking vs. Emotional Control

Positive thinking and emotional control are related—but they are not the same.

Positive thinking shapes **how you interpret** what happens.
Emotional control shapes **how you respond** to what happens.

Positive thinking says:
"This setback hurts, but I can learn from it."

Emotional control looks like:
Not sending the angry email you drafted in your head at 2:17 a.m.

One is internal meaning-making.
The other is external execution.

You can be optimistic and still reactive.
You can be realistic and deeply grounded.

Emotional control does not erase hard feelings.
It simply keeps them from hijacking your behavior.

Once you stop handing your emotions the keys, you unlock deeper strengths: resilience, flexibility, humility, and trust.

Presence over Positivity

When pressure hits, do you reach for forced optimism—or grounded presence? When regulation and mindset work together, you stop reacting to life and start shaping it.

Resilience: Respect It, but Do Not Rely on It

Resilience is often praised as a virtue—but too often, it is celebrated without examining what made it necessary in the first place.

We admire people who endure. Who absorb pressure. Who adapt, recover, and keep going even when depleted. But resilience is usually forged in environments that asked too much, offered too little, and expected survival to substitute for support. It is strength, yes—but it is frequently strength built in response to strain that could have been prevented.

Here is the uncomfortable distinction:
Resilience is reactive. It responds to harm. It does not prevent it.

When organizations, families, or systems lean too heavily on resilience, they quietly shift responsibility downward. The unspoken message becomes: *We will continue to apply pressure, and we trust you to withstand it.* Over time, this stops sounding like confidence and starts feeling like neglect.

Resilience should never be the price of belonging.

When people are continually praised for "handling it," "pushing through," or "being so strong," they learn something dangerous: their exhaustion is expected, their recovery is private, and their breaking point is theirs alone to manage. Burnout becomes normalized. Asking for help feels like failure. Rest becomes something you earn only after collapse.

And this is where cultures quietly erode.

People stop naming problems because they are proud of surviving them. They stop advocating for change because endurance has become identity. They stop imagining better because survival consumes all available energy.

Resilience keeps people alive in unhealthy systems.
It does not make those systems healthy.

True leadership does not ask people to be endlessly resilient—it works to make resilience less necessary. It designs environments that absorb stress before individuals must. It notices patterns of exhaustion and treats them as signals, not badges of honor.

The real test of a healthy culture is not how well people recover from burnout. It is how rarely they are pushed to the edge in the first place.

Honor resilience.
Respect the comeback.
But do not confuse endurance with excellence.

People deserve more than survival.
They deserve sustainability. They deserve space to thrive—not just prove they can withstand harm.

The Cost of Endurance

When did resilience stop feeling like strength and start feeling like survival? What would thriving look like if endurance were no longer the requirement?

Emotional Flexibility: The Next-Level Skill

Resilience survives disruption.
Emotional flexibility anticipates and navigates it.

Flexibility is the ability to adjust without losing yourself. To pivot without shattering. To take in new information and respond without defaulting to old scripts.

Where resilience often requires breakdown and recovery, emotional flexibility allows you to bend before breaking.

At work, flexibility looks like shifting from *"How do I survive this?"* to *"How can I adapt and still lead well here?"*

In relationships, it means releasing rigid expectations while maintaining boundaries. In life, it means seeing change as information and not attack.

Flexible thinking is not weak thinking.
It is strategic thinking.

It keeps your nervous system out of fight-or-flight and anchored in clarity.It allows you to respond rather than react, to lead with awareness rather than urgency.

The mastery is not surviving change—it is learning to move with it and still recognize yourself on the other side.

Get Humble Before You Are Humbled

There is a quiet truth about emotional regulation that rarely gets named: **Pride sabotages it faster than pressure ever will.**

Pride tells us we have arrived. That we already know. That feedback is for others—less seasoned, less capable, less evolved. Pride strengthens certainty and dulls curiosity. It narrows perspective until only our own viewpoint feels valid.

Pride is loud. Wisdom is quiet.

Humility, by contrast, is not weakness—it is emotional stability. It is the capacity to remain open when ego wants to close ranks. It is the willingness to ask, *"What am I missing?"* Even when you feel sure. *Especially* when you feel sure.

Getting humble before you are humbled is emotional insurance.

Because life has a way of correcting unchecked certainty. And when humility is absent, those corrections tend to be sharp, public, and painful. The fall hurts more not because the mistake was greater but because the ego had nowhere to land softly.

Humility does not mean shrinking yourself.
It does not mean surrendering authority.
It does not mean self-doubt masquerading as virtue.

It means staying teachable.

It means recognizing that being human means being fallible—and choosing awareness over defensiveness. It means noticing when confidence quietly hardens into certainty, when leadership turns into rigidity, when experience morphs into dismissal of other perspectives.

Humility keeps emotional flexibility alive.
It allows you to adjust without collapsing.
To receive feedback without imploding.
To remain grounded without becoming brittle.

The strongest leaders are not those who posture. They are the ones people trust with truth. The ones who can hear hard things without retaliating. The ones whose presence says, *"You can be honest here. I won't punish you for it."*

Humility creates psychological safety—not because it lowers standards, but because it lowers fear.

And here is the paradox:
The more grounded you are in humility, the more stable your authority becomes.

People do not follow those who need to be right.
They follow those who are willing to be real.

Humility refined.
Emotions regulated.
Presence intentional.

That is the soil where trust grows—and where leadership matures without hardening.

Confidence or Certainty?

Where might confidence have quietly tipped into certainty?
Notice where "I know" could soften into "I am still learning."
Humility does not weaken strength—it refines it.

The Trust Connection

When you develop emotional control, you do not just calm yourself—you expand your influence.

Calm becomes strategy. Clarity becomes your baseline.
Humility keeps ego from hijacking the moment.

You stop reacting from fear, urgency, or defensiveness and begin responding from wisdom and intention. That shift is not subtle. It changes how people experience you—and whether they feel safe, respected, and willing to follow your lead.

Trust is not accidental.
It is built choice by choice.

It is forged through emotional consistency, restraint, and alignment with values—especially in moments when it would be easier to react, withdraw, or assert power. Trust does not come from being impressive. It comes from being steady.

Real trust is never declared.
It is demonstrated.

It lives in your composure under pressure.
In your restraint during conflict.
In your willingness to pause instead of pounce.
Trust becomes visible through how you show up—not once, but repeatedly. And when emotional control guides your presence, trust stops being an outcome you chase and becomes the natural result of who you are.

That is leadership in its highest form.

And it is the bridge to what comes next.

Practicing Your Emotional Superpower

Power vs. Presence

When pressure rises, what guides you—
the need to be right or the desire to understand?
Power demands attention. Presence earns trust.

The Gift of Correction

How do you respond when someone offers you
honest feedback? Correction is not humiliation. It is an
invitation to grow steadier and more trustworthy.

The Living Proof of Integrity

Trust is not something you claim—it is something others feel
around you. Every calm response, every act of humility,
every moment of consistency plants the credibility
leadership depends on.

Part III: Strategy, Energy, and Daily Practices

Turning Self-Awareness Into Strategy, and Presence Into Power

By now, you have done real inner work.
You have learned how to quiet the noise, listen with intention, master your face, and choose your words with care. You have stopped shrinking, started pausing, and begun showing up on purpose.

Now it is time to turn that awareness into a way of life.

Because awareness without structure fades.
Emotional intelligence without boundaries burns you out.
Presence without strategy collapses under pressure.

This is where everything becomes sustainable.

This section is about translating insight into consistency—about protecting your energy, managing your focus, and building systems that support who you are becoming. Not by stacking routines for productivity's sake—by creating a daily architecture for your sanity so you can lead, think, and live from alignment instead of exhaustion.

You do not need more hacks.
You do not need more hustle.
You do not need another motivational slogan.

You need rhythm.
You need rest.
You need practices that keep your mind clear and your heart steady.

What comes next offers exactly that: the strategies, boundaries, and quiet disciplines that turn emotional intelligence from something you understand into something you live.

Because self-mastery is not a destination.
It is a daily practice.

And it is time to make it a habit.

Chapter 10:
Trust Is a Verb

Where Your Actions Do the Talking

Trust is not a vibe, a slogan, or a poster on the wall. It's not branding or a word you casually drop into meetings. **Trust is a verb.** It lives in movement—in choices, behaviors, and the subtle ways you show up.

Trust is built—and broken—in the ordinary, unglamorous moments: when you follow through exactly when you said you would; when you could disappear but choose to show up anyway; when you speak necessary truth instead of weaponizing silence. It is consistency. It is integrity. It is presence aligned with action. And yes, it often costs more than you expected.

Think of trust like a bank account. Every time you do what you said you would, you make a deposit. Every time you delay, deflect, avoid, or react impulsively, you make a withdrawal. And here is the uncomfortable truth: you rarely know which interaction will trigger the overdraft.

Trust is not something you announce. It is something you demonstrate. It is earned through the rhythm of your behavior, not the volume of your promises. It becomes visible in the quiet ways you move through the world—and in the reliability others come to depend on.

Show Up. Speak Up. Follow Through.

If trust is a verb, these are the moves that matter. They build credibility, shape culture, and turn leadership into something people can actually trust.

Show up.
Be present—physically, mentally, emotionally. Reliability is not glamorous, but it is unforgettable. People remember those who stay engaged when it would be easier not to.

Speak up.
Use your voice with clarity and courage. Say the honest thing without cruelty and the necessary thing without avoidance. Silence can be grounding when it is intentional or compassionate, but silence that avoids truth fractures trust more quietly than words ever could.

Follow through.
Deliver on what you commit to. Say less, deliver more. Consistency is the engine of trust, and nothing signals integrity more clearly than a promise kept on a Tuesday afternoon with no applause.

These three actions—showing up, speaking up, and following through—are simple, but rarely easy. They require emotional control, humility, and intention. Trust is not built in grand gestures; it is built through aligned choices, made again and again, especially when doing so is inconvenient.

The Trust Ledger

Where are you consistently making deposits—and where are you quietly overdrafting? Notice the gap between intention and impact. What one behavior could you shift today to close that gap?

Show Up: Where Ego Ends and Soul Begins

Showing up is more than being in the room. It is the moment ego steps aside and your real self arrives. Anyone can occupy a chair, nod at the right moments, and perform engagement. That is not showing up. That is going through the motions. True presence has weight. It signals: *I am here. I am listening. This matters.*

It is easy to confuse busyness with reliability, but busyness without engagement is just noise. You can attend every meeting and still leave people feeling unseen. Trust is built when your presence actually matters—when you come prepared, stay focused, and give others the dignity of your full attention. Showing up means following through without being chased and doing the work even when it is invisible or inconvenient.

This matters most in uncomfortable moments. When tension rises and conflict enters the room, that heat in your chest is not a signal to flee. It is information. Most people were never taught how to navigate conflict with steadiness. They were taught to avoid it, fear it, or overpower it. But conflict is not the enemy. An unchecked ego is.

Handled with emotional intelligence, disagreement becomes a doorway to understanding. It reveals values, needs, and unspoken expectations. Most conflicts are not about deadlines or email tone; they are about fairness, respect, acknowledgment, and belonging. Big emotions do not have to create big damage. When handled consciously, they create growth.

This is where ego gives way to soul.

Ego shows up to win.
Soul shows up to understand.
Ego reacts.
Soul reflects.
Ego escalates.
Soul listens.

In real moments, the difference is unmistakable.

Ego storms in, ready to prove a point.
Soul walks in asking, *"Help me understand what happened."*

Ego interrupts to defend.
Soul says, *"You're right. I missed that."*

Ego drafts a long email to justify.
Soul picks up the phone and says, *"Something feels off. Can we talk?"*

Ego hears disagreement as threat.
Soul hears it as information.

Ego keeps score.
Soul keeps perspective.

When you meet tension with curiosity instead of control, you create psychological safety—not the buzzword version, but the lived experience of being seen and respected even in disagreement. That safety is built through compassion, courage, and accountability practiced consistently over time.

Trust cannot grow where ego dominates. That is why humility—not hustle—is the quiet engine of trustworthy leadership. Humility allows you to say, *"I was wrong. Help me understand. I want to do better."*

Sometimes the strongest move is not a mic drop. It is silence. Not withdrawal, but reflective pause—the space where ego settles and clarity returns. Sometimes people do not need your explanation; they need your boundary. And sometimes showing up does not mean saying more. It means staying steady, staying human, and letting your presence speak.

Speak Up: Disagree Like a Grown-Up

Speaking up is the oxygen trust breathes.

Trust does not die from honest disagreement. It dies from silence—the brittle kind that fills a room when no one says what needs to be said. That silence is not neutral. It breeds confusion, resentment, and distance. When people do not feel safe to speak, trust suffocates. When they do speak and are dismissed, it collapses even faster.

Healthy teams do not exist because everyone agrees. They exist because people feel safe enough to tell the truth, challenge ideas, and raise concerns without fear of punishment or humiliation. Trust grows when people know they can speak honestly and still belong.

Speaking up is not about getting loud, dramatic, or cruel. It is about being real. Real with your observations. Real with your needs. Real with the people around you. The healthiest relationships—professional or personal—are not conflict-free. They are conflict-capable. They can handle disagreement with honesty, respect, and care.

We need a better definition of healthy. A healthy workplace is not one where no one disagrees. It is one where people know how to disagree well—challenging ideas without attacking people, expressing emotion without assigning blame, and addressing tension without lighting fires.

Disagreeing well is often simpler than we make it. It means naming tension early instead of letting it harden into resentment. It means saying, *"Something about that did not sit right with me—can we talk about it?"* instead of silently stewing or venting sideways. It means going directly to the person involved rather than triangulating through witnesses and group chats.

It also means staying present. Stay on topic. Do not resurrect old grievances. Speak for yourself rather than about others. *"I felt dismissed in that meeting,"* opens dialogue. *"You always ignore me,"* shuts it down.

The goal is not to win. It is to understand. To connect. To find alignment rather than dominance. That requires listening to understand, not listening to reload your next point. It requires curiosity when defensiveness wants control.

And sometimes the most responsible form of speaking up is restraint. Saying, *"I want to talk about this, but I need time to settle first,"* is not avoidance—it is wisdom. Timing matters. Emotional bandwidth matters.

Speaking up is not about volume. It is about clarity. Courage over comfort. Honesty over avoidance. Integrity over ego. Sometimes that courage looks like saying less. Sometimes it looks like asking one thoughtful question instead of delivering a speech.

Without shared norms—clear expectations for feedback, repair, and de-escalation—disagreement turns into chaos. With structure, it becomes progress. Healthy conflict stays focused on one issue, speaks directly, assumes good intent while holding accountability, and keeps dignity intact.

Trust grows when people know they can speak and still be respected. When disagreement is handled with maturity, tension becomes information rather than threat. The goal is never dominance—it is repair, clarity, and forward motion.

Because trust does not grow in silence.

It grows in honest conversation handled with care.
But even the best conversation means little without what comes next.

Follow Through: Where Trust Becomes Real

Follow-through is where trust becomes lived. You can show up and speak up, yet still fracture trust if you fail to follow through. This is where trust stops being conceptual and becomes lived. Without it, even courageous conversations dissolve into frustration and quiet resentment.

Follow-through is not just task completion—it is dependability. It means honoring agreements after emotions cool, not making people chase you for answers, and doing what you said you would do. It is answering the email you promised to answer, circling back when you said you would, and repairing what you damaged without being asked.

Trust is rarely built in grand moments. It grows through small, consistent, unglamorous choices—checking in before someone has to ask, admitting when you got something wrong, and correcting course without defensiveness. These steady acts turn conflict into resolution and resolution into trust.

The Mechanics of Follow-Through

Follow-through is where trust either strengthens or frays. Speaking up and naming truth matter—but none of it holds if your actions do not align afterward. This is where maturity, discipline, and self-awareness do their real work.

One of the biggest barriers to meaningful follow-through is responding to symptoms instead of causes. Tone may bother you, but what is underneath it? A missed deadline may signal a broken system, not indifference. Feeling dismissed may point to an unmet need or unspoken expectation.

Before acting, pause to ask:
- What is the real issue?
- How significant is the impact—honestly?
- What facts are clear, and where might assumptions be filling gaps?
- Who needs to be involved for resolution?
- What outcome would restore alignment?

These questions shift you from reaction to resolution. They prevent overcorrection, under-response, and misplaced responsibility.

Follow-through also requires emotional steadiness—the ability to separate fact from feeling while honoring both; to express needs without blame; to know when to pause, revisit, or release. It is not about forcing closure; it is about restoring understanding.

Trust does not require perfection.
It requires consistency.

And consistency is built through countless small acts of follow-through—done quietly, repeatedly, and with integrity.

Difficult Conversations Only Matter If They Move Us Forward

Speaking up builds trust only when what follows deepens respect, understanding, and repair. Difficult conversations create trust when they move us forward—not when they escalate, punish, or shut people down. Healthy conflict resolution requires four things: self-awareness, empathy, boundaries, and—before any of that—emotional regulation.

So here is the bonus round: Come to a full stop.

If you are emotionally flooded—heart racing, voice sharp, hands shaking—you are not in a place to build trust; you are in a place to break it. Step away. Breathe. Walk. Re-center. Return only when your nervous system has settled enough for your wisdom—not your ego—to be in charge.

Your conflict style often mirrors your trust patterns.

If you avoid conflict, you likely hope issues will resolve if you stay quiet. If you accommodate, you may keep the peace while resentment quietly builds. If you compete, you may need to be right, speak sharply, or dominate the room. If you compromise, you might settle for half-solutions no one feels good about.

Then there is cooperation—the gold standard. Cooperation is not about winning; it is about understanding. It is slower, sometimes it's messy, but it turns tension into progress and relationships into partnerships. It is where people listen before reacting, clarify before assuming, and co-create solutions that honor everyone in the room.

Trust thrives in environments where difficult conversations are respected, not avoided. High-trust teams do not tiptoe around tension—they meet it with transparency, structure, and emotional maturity.

Challenging interactions do not have to feel threatening. They can be collaborative, clarifying, and even—in the right hands—healing. When people know their voices matter and their dignity is safe, conflict becomes a place of possibility instead of fear.

There is no one-size-fits-all style, only the right approach for the right moment—and that begins with emotional literacy. If you avoid, name it. If you rush to solutions before understanding the problem, own it. If your volume rises when your anxiety spikes, recognize it. Self-awareness cracks open the door to trust; honesty keeps it open.

Once that door is open, the next essential step is learning how to repair—because even with the best intentions, we will still get it wrong sometimes.

Apologies, Forgiveness, and the Fine Art of Owning Your Mess

Let us talk about forgiveness—not the polished version people post online, but the real, grown-up kind. Forgiveness is not about letting someone else off the hook. It is about setting yourself free. Holding resentment is like dragging a carry-on full of emotional bricks: It is heavy. It is exhausting. And you are the one carrying it.

Forgiveness does not require reconciliation. It does not excuse what happened or grant renewed access to your energy. It simply means you are choosing not to keep carrying the poison.

You do not owe anyone forgiveness.
But you do owe yourself peace.

Now flip the script.

What happens when you are the one who caused the damage? You will—everyone does. Intentionally or not. This is where apology and accountability enter, and it is where many people stumble because they were never taught how to apologize like an actual adult.

A real apology is not a tactic.
It is courage.

It is not performative.
It is not emotional theater or a strategic dodge of responsibility.

It acknowledges impact, validates experience, and commits to repair. That is how trust begins to rebuild—through empathy paired with consistent action.

"I am sorry you feel that way," *sounds* polite but shifts blame to the other person's reaction.

A genuine apology sounds like:
"I am sorry that what I did made you feel dismissed. That was not my intention, but I recognize the impact."

"That is not what happened" rewrites reality.
A stronger response is:
"That is not how I remember it, but I hear that is how it felt—and that matters to me."

"You are overreacting" dismisses experience.
A healthier alternative:
"I did not intend to hurt you, but I can see that I did. Help me understand."

"I am the worst. I should just leave" centers shame.
A mature apology says:
"I handled that poorly. I am sorry. I want to make it right."

"Sorry" can open a door.
It cannot rebuild the house.

Only follow-through does that. Only steady behavior—not promises or sentiment—restores safety. Trust rebuilds through repetition and relability. It grows in patterns, not moments. In the quiet, consistent choices no one applauds but everyone remembers.

And forgiveness?
That is your liberation.
Not for them.
For you.

Embracing the Mess for the Sake of Growth

What if conflict were not something to fear, but something to engage? What if your next hard conversation was not a detour from progress but the doorway to it?

Conflict is messy, emotional, and deeply human. When we stop treating it as dysfunction and start seeing it as information, something shifts. Trust deepens. Communication sharpens. Ego loosens its grip. Growth becomes possible.

Trust is a verb. It is built in ordinary, inconvenient moments—the ones where it would be easier to look away, stay silent, or protect your pride. It is earned in how you show up when emotions run high, when your ego wants to defend, and your values ask you to pause.

This work is not about having it all figured out. It is about being real—taking responsibility, choosing consistency, and aligning your actions with your integrity, especially when things get uncomfortable.

So here is the challenge:

Show up.
Speak up.
Follow through.

Not just when it is easy.
Especially when it is hard.

Show Up. Speak Up. Follow Through. Trust Lives Here.

Trust is not branding or sentiment. It is behavior—proven through repeated choices, particularly under pressure.

Presence without honesty is empty.
Honesty without follow-through is hollow.
Consistency without awareness is blind.

Trust flourishes when all three move together.

Often, trust is built quietly. In steadiness. In pauses that de-escalate. In questions that invite rather than dominate. In leadership that does not need to be loud to be felt. This is the quiet strength of those who hold things together without seeking credit.

Sometimes the most powerful influence is not the most visible one. Sometimes trust looks like someone in the back of the room—steady, grounded, anchoring everyone else.

This is where leadership shifts from appearance to essence.
From performance to presence.
From intention to proof.

As we move forward—into deeper layers of influence, responsibility, and alignment—remember this:

Trust is not a title. It is evidence.

So show up.
Speak up.
Follow through.

Let your steadiness, your voice, and your integrity become the quiet proof of who you are.

Quiet Power

Ego or Soul?

When was the last time you showed up to understand
instead of to win? Ego seeks validation.
The soul seeks connection. Which one led your
last hard conversation?

The Grown-Up Test

When was the last time you entered a disagreement with
curiosity instead of armor? Speaking up well is not about
being right—it is about being real, respectful, and
willing to stay in the room.

The Courage to Repair

Where might a sincere apology rebuild something that pride
has kept distant? What would it cost you to say, "I see the
impact—and I care enough to make it right?"

Chapter 11:
Hidden Genius — The Quiet Power of the Unseen Strategists

Where Influence Goes When It Stops Needing Attention

Not all leadership is loud.
Not all power is visible.
And not all brilliance announces itself.

As we move deeper into the work of strategy, alignment, and daily practice, it becomes essential to name a truth many people feel but rarely articulate: Some of the most impactful leaders operate quietly, thoughtfully, and often without recognition. They do not dominate a room—they stabilize it. They do not chase attention—they direct it toward what matters. They do not perform—they sustain.

This chapter is for them.

And possibly...for you.

The Ones Who Hold Everything Together

Let us pause to honor a group of people who rarely receive the credit they deserve, yet often hold entire teams, families, and ecosystems together: the quietly brilliant, emotionally intelligent, high-capacity humans. They do not seek the spotlight or ask for applause. Yet their steady contribution is often the difference between chaos and calm, failure and success, stagnation and movement.

These are the hidden strategists—the intuitive thinkers and pattern-seers who notice what others overlook. They process complexity without theatrics, anticipate problems before they surface, and read both people and systems with remarkable fluency. While others debate step two, they have already mapped step ten and quietly placed the guardrails that keep everything intact.

They function as an internal compass—unofficial, often unacknowledged, yet consistently essential. Many learned early to stay small to avoid unnecessary risk. Standing out once meant standing alone, so they mastered influence without ego, leadership without title, and impact without noise.

The environments they inhabit—at work, at home, in community—often feel steady not because they are distant, but because they serve as structural supports for everything around them. They anchor emotional climates, reinforce systems, and stabilize relationships with a reliability most people do not fully recognize until it is gone.

They build culture from the inside out.

For them, purpose and values are not abstract language; they are guiding forces. When they commit, they do so with depth. Their passion does not perform—it hums. Their influence emerges not through self-promotion but through how they speak, how they serve, and how they quietly model what they believe.

They are the peacekeepers, the temperature-readers, the early-warning systems—the steady stabilizers who sense morale shifting before anyone else names it. They detect widening tension, looming failure, or unspoken support needs long before they become visible. They remember the last time a "brilliant idea" collapsed—because they were the ones left carrying its impact.

Their strength lives in service, not spectacle. Their loyalty is sincere. Others rely on them instinctively. In high-stakes moments, their steadiness becomes the anchor.

What makes them exceptional is not only their capability, but their orientation. They understand their purpose and execute with precision. When alignment shifts or a season ends, they leave with grace—not turbulence, resentment, or noise. They know when to sustain and when to release.

Most profoundly, they possess an intuition that resists measurement. They sense undercurrents others miss and recognize patterns before they fully form. Offer them trust, space, and autonomy and they will quietly transform a team—or a life—in ways that are often revealed only in hindsight.

Too often, their impact is misunderstood. Because they do not demand attention, they are underestimated. Because they do not push to be heard, they may be mistaken for passive. Yet these are the anchors in the storm—the translators between turbulence and steadiness, the unseen strategists whose quiet intelligence defines true leadership.

Ignore them, and foundations weaken.
Notice them, empower them, and you will witness the discernment, strength, and stabilizing power that has been holding everything together all along.

This is where influence evolves into something deeper: leadership without noise, power without ego, and visibility no longer dependent on volume.

The One Holding the Structure

Who is the hidden strategist in your life—the one whose steadiness quietly keeps everything upright? What has their presence taught you about leadership that never needs applause?

The Paradox of Invisibility

Some individuals hold organizations, families, and entire communities together without ever raising their voice. They sense tension before it escalates. They catch system glitches before they become crises. They notice subtle rifts in team dynamics long before they erupt into conflict. Their genius lies in prevention, not recovery—and that is precisely why it is so often overlooked.

When a fire is prevented, no one applauds.
When a fire is extinguished, people cheer.

Quiet strategists do not shout, grandstand, or clamor for attention. They simply get it done—calmly, consistently, reliably. They stabilize rooms not by dominating them but by communicating something essential through presence alone: This is under control. We will get through this.

That same steadiness, however, can unsettle insecure leaders. Not because these strategists seek power, but because their competence exposes gaps others would rather ignore. Instead of rising to meet the challenge, some leaders minimize, dismiss, or quietly undermine the very people holding everything together.

That is the paradox. The qualities that make these individuals indispensable—humility, foresight, composure—also make them easy to overlook. They do not demand credit, so they often do not receive it. They do not insist on authority, so it may never be granted. Yet their influence shapes outcomes far more than titles ever could.

Meanwhile, chaos continues around them. A small oversight snowballs into a multi-department mess. Processes stall. Tempers rise. While others scramble, the strategist is already several layers deep into the solution. They do not compete for attention or hoard recognition. They simply reset the system—again.

But there is a cost.

Reliability without recognition has consequences.

Brilliance expressed quietly is mistaken for background noise. Foresight is dismissed until repeated by someone louder. A measured approach is misread as apathy. Patience is confused for weakness. And when work remains consistently unseen, a distortion sets in—they begin to question whether their value exists at all.

This is invisibility at its sharpest: the people who keep the scaffolding intact become the ones doubting their own brilliance. Not because they lack confidence—because the silence surrounding their contribution grows louder than the contribution itself.

Yet absence of applause is not absence of impact. Quiet genius does not stop being genius simply because others fail to recognize it. Invisibility is sometimes strategy, sometimes survival, and sometimes the only reason the system has not collapsed.

Self-Recognition Is Not Vanity

*What acknowledgment do you need to offer yourself today
for work no one ever sees? Self-recognition is not ego—
it is restoration.*

The Consequences of a Good Heart

Hidden strategists do not merely solve problems—they are committed to preventing them. Their drive comes as much from heart as from intellect. They build, they contribute, they connect. They give because generosity is part of their wiring. Yet here lies the tension: not everyone moves through the world with that same depth. Some show up to compete, to extract, to win.

When you lead with empathy and integrity, you will inevitably encounter people who mistake kindness for weakness, patience for indifference, and calm for complacency. The temptation is to harden in response—to trade generosity for cynicism, steadiness for bitterness.

But that is not strength. That is surrender.

Empathy is not naïve—it is mastery.
Calm is not indifference—it is strength under control.
Integrity does not become optional simply because others have abandoned theirs or refused to see yours.

The cost of a good heart is that you feel more. You invest fully, and when others show up half-hearted—or with hidden agendas—it stings. You give your best and still go unnoticed. You pour yourself out, and others assume the supply is endless. They take because they believe they must. You give because that is who you are.

And still, you do not trade it in.

Because the true test of character is refusing to become what hurts you. It is resisting the urge to shrink your generosity to match someone else's scarcity. It is choosing not to retaliate in ways that betray your own values. A strategist's power lies in staying soft without becoming naïve, in holding empathy without dropping boundaries, in remaining aligned even in misaligned environments.

Yes, people will misunderstand. They will think your restraint means you do not feel their urgency. They will mistake kindness for complacency. They will read steadiness as incapacity.

Let them.

Their misunderstanding does not rewrite your character. Their smallness does not diminish your strength. You do not need to convince shallow minds of your worth, nor contort yourself to fit their comfort.

Staying soft in a world determined to harden you is not weakness—it is wisdom. It is not passivity—it is grounded alignment. Do not dim your light because it unsettles someone squinting in the dark. Do not betray your heart to match the temperature of a room never designed for you.

This is where emotional resilience meets strategic intelligence. Quiet strategists know that silence can be strength, that stillness can be action, and that withdrawal can be the most strategic move of all. When they disengage, it is not because they lack ideas—it is because they have stopped wasting energy being unheard.

High-capacity individuals are often humble to a fault. They will not wave their brilliance around. They do not need applause to keep contributing. But humility must never be mistaken for insignificance. When their contributions suddenly stop, it is not an accident—it is a signal. Their energy did not disappear. It moved to a place where it will be respected.

And here is the final paradox: The same heart that makes them indispensable also makes them willing to walk away with their integrity intact—the strength to feel deeply, to be overlooked, to hurt, and still choose alignment. The wisdom to leave quietly, knowing they never had to trade their soul for recognition.

That is the consequence of a good heart: to carry more weight, to feel more deeply, and to rest more peacefully knowing you never had to abandon yourself to survive.

Empathy with Edges

Where does your empathy need a boundary—not to harden you, but to keep you whole? Wisdom is compassion that knows when to pause.

Why High-Capacity People Struggle

High-capacity people do not struggle because they are "too much." They struggle because most environments are built for the middle—middle speed, middle insight, middle ambition—and they are anything but.

While others are easing their way from point A to point B, high-capacity thinkers have already mapped the route, optimized the workflow, and solved the four problems no one else has noticed yet.

Meanwhile, chaos masquerades as collaboration.

Rhonda in Finance has stalled the workflow mid-click. Seven departments are spiraling. And you—emotionally attuned, quietly brilliant, carrying the psychic weight of ten people—are wondering if you are somehow the problem, crying into your coffee, questioning every life choice that led you here.

Here is the truth:
You are not the problem.

The problem is that excellence is often inconvenient in environments designed for comfort. Drive gets labeled excessive. Insight gets dismissed as difficult. High standards are framed as unrealistic or a failure to "understand complexity" when in truth, they are simply... standards.

Instead of mentorship or autonomy, high-capacity people are often met with micromanagement and subtle containment. Let us name this clearly: **Micromanaging a high-capacity thinker is a socially acceptable form of workplace bullying.** It delivers one unmistakable message: *"I do not trust you"*—even when trust has been earned a thousand times over.

High-capacity individuals are not seeking power or control. They want freedom—the space to think, build, and solve without being slowed by bottlenecks, bureaucracy, or brittle egos. Yet many leaders misinterpret excellence as competition. The ability of someone who can do in two hours what others drag across two weeks exposes a gap—and instead of rising to meet it, some tighten the reins.

For the unseen strategist, this dynamic is exhausting.

Not because the work is hard—because the work is harder than it needs to be.

They see the simple path yet must navigate misalignment, outdated processes, fragile egos, and endless explanations to people who may never understand. Explaining logic to someone who resists it is not collaboration— it is erosion.

And when erosion continues unchecked, something shifts.

Quietly.
Subtly.
With graceful, strategic inevitability.

The mind stays sharp.
The effort withdraws.
The brilliance begins looking for air.

Used Isn't the Same as Valued

Where has your brilliance been relied upon but not protected?
Exhaustion is not weakness—it is information.

When the Fire Starts to Dim

High-capacity people rarely burn out dramatically.

Their exhaustion is quiet. Precise. Almost surgical.

One day, their SOPs are impeccably updated.
Their calendar becomes suspiciously clean.
They stop catching every dropped ball.
They let small mistakes slide—the ones they used to fix before anyone else even knew they existed.

This is not disengagement born of apathy.
It is disengagement born of recognition.

They have entered the wind-down season.

Their effort does not disappear; it redirects—to a place where it will be respected. And most organizations never recover from this shift because by the time it is noticed, the strategist is already rehearsing the exit. Not in anger. Not in chaos. In grace.

Carrying brilliance in environments that misunderstand excellence creates a very specific kind of fatigue. Competence is treated like a threat instead of a gift. They hold the torch while everyone else forgets there is even a fire.

And when these same strategists are asked to "train others," the exhaustion compounds. Training is not arrogance—it is math. Teaching someone who does not care costs more energy than quietly fixing it yourself.

Remote and hybrid work only amplify the problem. When effort becomes invisible, invisible labor—anticipating, preventing, correcting—becomes easier to overlook. The quiet strategist keeps compensating until the cost finally outweighs the commitment.

This is why high-capacity people interrupt.
Finish sentences.
Move quickly.

Not because they are rude—because they are already there, five steps ahead, map in hand, contingency plans drafted.

And if they ever stop being there?

You have already lost them.

If you are fortunate enough to have one of these minds on your team, protect them—not with coddling, but with respect. Respect their pace. Respect their insight. Respect their boundaries. Challenge them thoughtfully. Trust them deeply. Value them consistently.

And for the love of workflow—do not make Rhonda their problem.

High-capacity people do not struggle because they are "too much." They struggle because the environments around them are too limited.

When you learn to support—and unleash—their brilliance?

Everything changes.

Coaching the Quiet Strategist

Even the most capable and emotionally intelligent strategists need support. They carry enormous weight—much of it unseen—and without a place to reflect, even the strongest minds can falter. The best leaders, mentors, and partners understand this. They do not rush to fix or direct. They create space, extend trust, and hold a mirror up to brilliance that rarely pauses long enough to see itself.

Coaching a quiet strategist is less about instruction and more about attentiveness. It is the art of noticing without intruding, of asking instead of answering, of listening for what is unspoken rather than what is obvious. Some scholars call this *coaching with compassion* (Boyatzis, Smith & Van Oosten, 2019), but the essence is simple: often the most powerful coaching moment is silence—allowing the strategist to unwind complexity on their own terms. Guidance becomes oxygen—felt more than seen.

These individuals thrive on challenge, not chaos. They want autonomy supported by structure and accountability anchored in trust. They crave clarity, innovation, and purpose—and resist micromanagement with every fiber of their being. They are acutely sensitive to environments that protect comfort over excellence. Effective coaching helps them use those instincts as tools rather than armor.

Even at the highest levels, quietly brilliant strategists still need sounding boards. The higher one rises, the fewer safe places exist for unfiltered perspective. In difficult moments, they do not look to titles—they look to steady, emotionally attuned people whose influence runs deeper than hierarchy. The untitled leaders. The stabilizers. The ones whose presence restores order without needing to command it.

These stabilizers are often the gatekeepers of trust within any system. If they are misaligned, everything downstream feels it. They read emotional temperature, timing, and subtext with fluency. They know the difference between resistance and fear, enthusiasm and performance, alignment and compliance. They do not simply support change—they translate it.

With the right environment—one that offers breathing room, creativity, and genuine trust—quiet strategists become some of the most transformative leaders in any setting. Their impact may never appear on dashboards, but it is evident in the steadiness of the team, the health of the culture, and the quiet hum of systems that simply work.

For coaches and mentors, the first requirement is self-awareness. Coaching demands emotional neutrality—the ability to see patterns without projecting onto them. It requires knowing how you show up, when to speak, and when to stay still. Sometimes the most effective intervention is restraint. Silence has a way of surfacing truths that language can obscure.

There is truth in the saying that coaches often "coach people out of their jobs." People seek coaching when something in them is ready for more—more alignment, more truth, more challenge, or more peace. Coaching becomes the bridge between who they have been and who they are becoming. And often, that next chapter leads somewhere new.

Not everyone is ready for that work. Some seek coaching when what they truly need is therapy. Others want growth—until growth requires discomfort. Skilled coaches recognize the difference and meet people where they are, without force or judgment.

Here is the quieter truth: Even coaches need coaches. One marker of effective coaching is that the coach feels grounded and energized afterward (Boyatzis, Smith & Beveridge, 2013). Holding emotional space is heavy work. Without support, the coach becomes the strategist without fuel—composed, competent, and quietly depleted.

The same is true for strategists themselves. Their environments often feel calm and contained because they are the ones regulating the system. Beneath that serenity is someone holding the emotional temperature of many—keeping things steady without ever being asked if they need rest.

Good coaching interrupts that pattern. It reminds the strategist that strength does not require isolation. It offers language for what they feel, structure for what they carry, and permission to rest without guilt. The goal is not to make them louder, flashier, or more visible. The goal is balance—so they remain steady, connected, and whole without losing their center.

Support for the Supporter

Who supports you the way you support everyone else?
Even the strong need a place where they do not have to be strong.

Recognizing and Retaining High-Capacity Thinkers

Autonomy, Freedom, and Strategic Presence

Hidden genius thrives on freedom—not chaos. Purposeful, structured freedom. Creative freedom. Strategic freedom. Intellectual freedom. High-capacity thinkers need room to think differently, space to speak honestly, and autonomy to innovate intuitively. When those conditions disappear, motivation does not explode—it erodes. Slowly. Quietly. And often unnoticed until it is too late.

This is not laziness.
This is clarity.
This is self-respect asserting itself.

When environments honor their contribution, high-capacity thinkers are generous with their time, insight, creativity, and energy. But when micromanagement, mistrust, or politics creep in, resentment spreads silently and destructively. Excellence cannot survive where autonomy is punished.

High performers want transparency, clearly defined responsibility, and systems that respect contribution. When one person consistently carries the load while others collect the accolades, you will lose your best people—and you will not get them back. Not loudly. Not dramatically. Precisely.

That is why organizations must protect standards as fiercely as they celebrate success. High-capacity contributors do not flourish in preventable chaos. You cannot demand brilliance while scrutinizing every move. You cannot expect innovation while tightening control. You cannot sustain excellence without coherence.

The solution is not more rules.
Not more layers.
Not more oversight.

The solution is awareness.

Stop patching systemic wounds with performative quick fixes.
Stop holding emergency meetings about problems that were obvious months ago.
Start listening to the people who have been quietly naming the truth all along.

Real thinkers do not crave applause—they crave progress. They do not need more meetings—they need more trust. They are not seeking control—they are trying to repair what is broken. So give them space. Stop managing their minutes and start valuing their outcomes.

Do not confuse steadiness with passivity. Just because someone is not loud does not mean they are not leading. Some of the most decisive leadership moments happen in silence—through deep thought, pattern recognition, and commitment to the long game.

High-capacity thinkers do not merely complete tasks.
They build systems.
They strengthen environments.
They reroute workflows.
They stabilize climates.

But they will only do so where they feel valued—and seen.

Create room for complexity. Invite nuance. Trust your thinkers. And, most importantly, listen to the ones already holding the fort. They may not seek credit. They may not want the spotlight. But they are quietly building the future. All they need is space to breathe—and the freedom to create without apology.

Fail to recognize them and you will see burnout, disengagement, and attrition. When they leave, it is rarely chaotic. It is clean. Their energy simply moves elsewhere, and the organization is left wondering why everything suddenly feels heavier.

But when you recognize, empower, and protect them?

You do not just retain talent.
You unlock foresight, innovation, and stability that no bureaucracy can manufacture.

Stewardship, Not Control

Where might loosening the reins—without lowering standards— allow someone else to rise? Trust is often the oxygen high-capacity people have been working without.

The Hidden Geniuses in Your Orbit

These are the unseen strategists—the quiet powerhouses who do not clamor for attention yet command deep respect. They do not need credit; they need alignment and shared understanding. And when they receive it, they bring oxygen to rooms that did not realize they were suffocating.

While others fight for the microphone, they scan the environment—reading dynamics, mapping risks, and creating order out of chaos. Not for ego. Not for validation. Because they care about outcomes, integrity, and purpose. They are silent anchors, steadying teams with emotional intelligence, strategic vigilance, and a humility so consistent it often goes unnoticed.

The most powerful influence is not always the most visible. Sometimes it is the steadiness you barely register—until you imagine what would collapse without it.

And if you find yourself bristling in their presence, pause.
Ask yourself: *What exactly is my ego protecting?*

Ego whispers: *They are outshining me.*
Soul replies: *They are helping us grow.*

Ego clings to control.
Soul seeks excellence.

There is a profound difference between being in control and creating an environment where control is no longer necessary. The strongest leaders understand this—and choose the latter.

If you want sustainability, stop playing it safe. Stop hiring for predictability when what you actually need is brilliance. Stop designing systems that protect mediocrity at the expense of excellence.

Hidden strategists thrive where complexity is welcomed and original thinking is encouraged. When you trust them, you do not simply get better answers—you get better questions.

Make room for the deep thinkers. Invite nuance. Empower the people quietly holding the seams together. They may not want the spotlight. They may never ask for attention. But do not mistake their lack of noise for lack of impact.

They are steadily building the future—while others are still busy proving themselves.

Guarding the Guardians: Recognizing the Shadows

Even as hidden strategists anchor teams, families, and entire systems, counterforces are always at play—energy drains, emotional leeches, and personalities whose presence destabilizes more than it strengthens. For every calm architect holding the structure together, someone (sometimes several someones) is loosening bolts, stirring tension, or siphoning energy without ever acknowledging the cost.

This is not cynicism.
It is discernment.

High-capacity, emotionally attuned people carry enormous weight. They sense what others miss, repair what others break, and stabilize what others never realized was wobbling. But without protection, their brilliance is slowly eroded—worn down by chaos, manipulation, and the relentless expectation that they will keep compensating for what others refuse to hold.

And that is the real danger.

Not that hidden strategists will fail—
but that they will quietly fade.

Not because they are weak,
but because they were never meant to operate unshielded.

Hidden strategists build futures.
Their genius may be quiet, but their influence is structural.

Preserving their strength—and the health of any system they sustain—requires recognizing the forces that erode shared understanding, corrode morale, and fracture cohesion. It requires naming what drains them, interrupts them, and feeds off their steadiness.

Protecting the guardians is not optional.

It is essential if we want environments where brilliance thrives, where clarity is honored, emotional labor is valued, and the people who hold everything together are no longer asked to sacrifice themselves to do so.

The Quiet Powerhouses

A Moment of Protection

Who protects the protectors—the ones who steady the room and rarely ask for anything in return? Notice where their brilliance is being drained. Guard the guardians; their stability holds everything together.

A Moment of Boundaries

Where have you been absorbing dysfunction simply because you can? Name one place where capability has been mistaken for endless availability. Strength is choosing what you will no longer carry.

A Moment of Discernment

Which dynamics repeatedly drain your clarity, confidence, or peace? Patterns matter. Your genius thrives where your energy is respected—and withers where it is consumed.

Chapter 12:
Soul Suckers, Energy Vampires, & Emotional Leeches

"Do not let the behavior of others destroy your inner peace."

– Dalai Lama

The Soul Suckers Exist

There are people whose presence strengthens a room—and others who drain it. Not because they are flawed (we all are) but because their patterns consume emotional space, distort clarity, and steal time while offering little stability, respect, or reciprocity in return.

To anchor this, let's name the behaviors:

Soul Suckers: People who steadily erode dignity, morale, or emotional steadiness through manipulation, negativity, or control.

Energy Vampires: Those who feed on attention and reaction—thriving on drama, chaos, crisis, and emotional labor.

Emotional Leeches: People who attach to capable, compassionate humans and drain them under the guise of need, loyalty, insecurity, or dependence.

These are not diagnoses or character assassinations.
They are descriptions of impact. And the impact is real.

We've all encountered them—the colleague whose entrance changes the room, the friend who turns every conversation into heavy lifting, the leader who disguises control as guidance while quietly eroding trust. Left unchecked, these dynamics siphon focus, time, and emotional reserves until exhaustion starts to feel inevitable.

Here's the important truth:
Every human being has the capacity to grow.
But not everyone will.
And certainly not on your timeline.

Two people can meet the same individual and walk away with different experiences—one sees potential; the other feels depleted. Both can be true. Growth capacity and emotional impact are not mutually exclusive.

So, let's ground this in something essential:
Access to your energy is a privilege, not a right.

Your attention, time, and emotional availability are valuable resources. You are responsible for stewarding them wisely. When someone treats you as a dumping ground, a stage for unresolved tension, or a place to extract stability without offering any in return, it is time to pause and reevaluate proximity.

Not everyone deserves access.
Even fewer have earned sustained attention.
And almost no one deserves unlimited emotional capacity.

This is not judgment.
It is discernment.
It is emotional stewardship.
It is protecting your clarity so you can lead, love, and live without depletion as your baseline.

Energy Does Not Lie

Where does your body tighten the moment a certain person enters the room? Where does your spirit feel smaller instead of steadier? Your nervous system recognizes truth long before your logic can justify it.

The Anatomy of Soul Suckers

Soul suckers don't all look alike. Some announce themselves through obvious chaos: the loud complainer; the chronic drama generator; the person whose presence instantly demands attention, emotional labor, and patience. Every interaction exacts a toll on focus and calm.

Others are subtler—cloaked in charm, courtesy, or "support." Consider the boss who praises you publicly while undermining you behind closed doors. Or the friend who insists they're "helping you think things through," yet leaves you doubting yourself after every conversation.

The goal isn't to memorize a catalog of toxic behaviors. It's to recognize patterns.

Most soul suckers fall into two broad archetypes: **overt chaos agents** and **covert polished saboteurs**. Chaos agents drain loudly—dramatic, reactive, exhausting. Polished saboteurs drain quietly—composed, socially skilled, harder to detect because you feel the shift in your energy long before you can prove it on paper.

Recognizing the difference helps you anticipate behavior, respond with intention, and protect your capacity before depletion takes hold.

Overt Soul Suckers: Chaos Agents

Chaos agents are easy to identify because they don't hide. They thrive on disorder and feed on the energy created when others scramble to compensate. In organizations, they often surface as leaders who cannot tolerate competence. Anyone too capable, organized, or respected is treated as a threat. Minor issues become crises, projects are reinvented unnecessarily, and feigned confusion is rarely accidental—it's strategic.

Colleagues can play the same game. Chronic tardiness, disorganization, and missed deadlines recalibrate an entire team's expectations. When these behaviors go unaddressed, chaos spreads. Competent people pick up the slack until burnout, disengagement, or attrition takes hold. Over time, the exception becomes the norm—dysfunction becomes "just how it is."

Chaos isn't limited to the workplace. It shows up in families, friendships, and partnerships: the relative who hijacks every gathering, the friend whose life is one perpetual emergency, the partner who thrives on drama. Tension gets normalized until calm starts to feel unfamiliar.

With chaos agents, peace is rarely sustainable. Their nervous system is calibrated to manage noise and they pull others into it to keep the system alive or functioning.

Covert Soul Suckers: Polished Saboteurs

If chaos agents drain loudly, polished saboteurs drain quietly. They cloak manipulation in charm, warmth, politeness, or "concern." Outwardly, they seem supportive and aligned. Behind the scenes, they undermine with precision—leaving you replaying conversations, second-guessing yourself, and feeling inexplicably depleted.

They don't disrupt the room.
They reshape it until confusion feels like your fault.

Polished saboteurs thrive where appearance matters more than substance. They publicly celebrate contributions while privately minimizing them. They endorse innovation, then quietly repurpose the work as their own. They present as gracious while tightening emotional pressure points.

And when they're in leadership?
They don't yell.
They destabilize.

They default to the familiar playbook of insecure leadership:
- Withold acknowledgment of wins while magnifying small mistakes.
- Offer feedback you can't use—until uncertainty becomes your baseline.
- Slowly shrink your authority while keeping your responsibility intact.

One day you notice it: Your scope has narrowed, but the pressure hasn't.

That isn't accidental.
That imbalance is by design.

In personal life, the pattern is just as slippery. A friend who "helps you think clearly" leaves you doubting yourself. A sibling offers praise wrapped in critique. A partner alternates comfort with guilt. The outcome is the same: disorientation. You stay tethered to relationships that appear supportive while steadily draining you.

Polished saboteurs provoke—then retreat into victimhood. When confronted, they recast you as the aggressor. Unlike chaos agents who leave visible wreckage, polished saboteurs erode confidence slowly—rewriting emotional reality until depletion feels familiar... and invisible.

The Subtle Undermining

Who in your life turns simple exchanges into emotional storms you ever created? Trust what your body recognizes before your mind talks you out of it.

Recognizing the Drain

Whether overt or covert, soul suckers leave a measurable imprint on mind and body: the knot in your stomach before you see them, the urge to over-explain simple decisions, the restless replay of conversations long after they end. These aren't quirks. They're signals that your energy is being siphoned and your boundaries are being tested.

The cycle is predictable: confusion, guilt, frustration, anger, and, eventually, detachment. What's unfolding is rarely connection—it's a power exchange. Burnout doesn't always come from doing too much. It comes from doing emotional labor in the wrong system, for the wrong people, under expectations that were never aligned.

The earliest signs are often small: a comment that makes you question your judgment, a moment that quietly transfers responsibility to you, a "minor" exchange that leaves you deflated. Over time, these extractions accumulate like termites—weakening the beams. Naming them early restores agency, reinforces boundaries, and protects your capacity before anything collapses.

Reclaiming energy isn't selfish—it's strategic. Recognizing the drain is how calm, competent, high-capacity people remain steady even when others are determined to pull everything off balance.

__Patterns over Excuses__

*What recurring pattern leaves you drained after being generous?
Energy does not leak by accident—it leaks through systems.*

Culture and Consequences

The behavior of a few individuals ripples outward, shaping environments far beyond their immediate actions. As Gruenert and Whitaker wrote (2015), "The culture of any organization is shaped by the worst behavior a leader is willing to tolerate." This applies far beyond workplaces. It applies to families, friendships, communities—every shared space we inhabit. Mission statements, values, and intentions matter far less than daily practice.

When leaders ignore immaturity, when peers enable manipulation, when friends quietly look away...dysfunction becomes normalized. Silence writes its own rulebook.

Over time, everyone learns what is acceptable here. What begins as one person's destructive behavior metastasizes into a collective standard. Awareness is not paranoia; it is protection. Recognizing these dynamics allows you to safeguard your energy, preserve motivation, and prevent the slow erosion of trust, morale, and cohesion.

Soul suckers often thrive in environments shaped by confusion, inconsistency, and imbalance. They are not always malicious; many operate unconsciously, unaware of the emotional extraction embedded in their behavior. But the impact is the same—intentional or not. Recognizing these behavioral patterns is not about blame; it is about reclaiming agency. Awareness creates the possibility for boundaries, restores emotional groundedness, and preserves forward momentum.

Which leads to an essential question:

What exactly are these soul suckers made of—and how do they operate within the spaces we share? Understanding their patterns is the key to neutralizing their influence without sacrificing your own energy in the process.

Silence Is a Culture

Where has silence replaced accountability in your environment? Culture shifts the moment someone chooses honesty over comfort. Let that someone be you.

The Antidote

The antidote to soul suckers is not confrontation for confrontation's sake.
It is steadiness.
It is detachment.

Detachment is not coldness or indifference. It is the refusal to pour emotional labor into dysfunction. It allows you to observe what is happening without being pulled into it—protecting your peace through intention rather than defensiveness.

In professional settings, detachment looks like holding clear expectations, setting firm boundaries, and refusing to serve as the perpetual clean-up crew for someone else's chaos. In personal life, it may mean letting the guilt-laden call go to voicemail, stepping out of manufactured crises, or naming manipulation for what it is—even when it arrives wrapped in courtesy or "concern."

Detachment is an act of self-respect.
It is the disciplined practice of conserving peace while refusing the bait.

Accountability, however, cannot be imposed from the outside. True accountability must rise from within. What you can do is model integrity, set consistent standards, and allow others to choose: rise to them—or reveal their unwillingness to grow.

Recognizing the spectrum—from overt chaos agents to subtle, polished saboteurs—gives you leverage. You learn to spot the drain before it pulls you under, respond with steadiness instead of reactivity, and reclaim agency over where your energy goes. Awareness may not eliminate dysfunction overnight, but it restores your power to decide who earns access to you.

Misplaced empathy and conflict avoidance often intensify these dynamics. Leaders who fear discomfort—and peers who confuse compassion with enablement—tolerate chaos in the name of "harmony," unknowingly rewarding dysfunction. The result is predictable: mediocrity is protected, high performers are depleted, and resentment quietly grows.

This pattern is not confined to work. It shows up in families, friendships, and partnerships—the sibling who guilt-trips, the friend in perpetual crisis, the partner whose chaos repeatedly spills into calm spaces because boundaries are never enforced. Tolerating these dynamics does not preserve harmony; it preserves imbalance.

Your responsibility is not to control others. You cannot manufacture maturity or force self-awareness. But you can safeguard your environment by safeguarding your energy. Define what is acceptable. Uphold it consistently. Follow through. Then practice strategic detachment—withdraw emotional labor from those who repeatedly choose chaos over responsibility.

By setting the standard—and holding it with calm conviction—you become a stabilizing force in environments that might otherwise drift toward dysfunction. You protect the conditions where high performers thrive, where culture remains healthy, and where chaos is no longer subsidized by your steadiness.

Detach to Return

Where is detachment needed—not to punish others, but to return to yourself? Boundaries do not create distance from others. They create proximity to your own peace.

Boundaries

The cure for soul suckers is not confrontation alone.
It is boundaries.

Boundaries are not walls; they are standards. They are the invisible lines that quietly, consistently declare: This is acceptable. That is not. They protect your time, energy, and emotional capacity—not through drama or defense but through clarity.

Boundaries are not reactive.
They are intentional.
They are steady.

Think of personal space like a hula hoop: you control its distance, its movement, and its access. You decide who enters, how close they come, and under what conditions you engage. Boundaries are not a one-time announcement; they are a daily practice—unseen, reliable, and essential to emotional hygiene.

In practice, boundaries sound simple—but they carry weight:
- You may sit at my table, but you do not get to flip it.
- I will not explain myself to someone committed to misunderstanding me.
- My peace is not collateral for your chaos.

These are not threats.
They are not ultimatums.
They are declarations.

Each one signals self-respect without hostility. Empathy without boundaries is not compassion—it is self-erasure. Time, attention, and emotional presence are finite resources. Protecting them is not selfish; it is survival. It is how high-capacity people remain grounded instead of depleted.

Boundaries also function as a diagnostic tool. They reveal who respects you—and who benefits from your lack of resistance. If someone responds to your limits with anger, guilt, or indignation, the boundary has already done its work. It has exposed the truth of the relationship.

If enforcing boundaries casts you as the villain in someone's narrative, accept it. You are not cruel—you are clear. You are not cold—you are disciplined. You are refusing to subsidize dysfunction with your energy.

Boundaries do not require consensus.
They do not need explanation.
They demand consistency.

When upheld daily, boundaries transform chaos into order, drama into calm, and depletion into sustainable presence. They are the quiet declaration that your energy belongs to you—and you choose how it is spent.

Aligned, Not Available

Where is your life asking for a firmer no?
Alignment is not about being less generous—it is about being
more loyal to yourself.

Graceful Exits and Gut Punches

Sometimes the truth arrives as a gut punch:
You cared more than they did.

You showed up—consistently, thoughtfully, with intention. You invested energy, attention, and emotional labor, believing it was mutual. And then, quietly, the reality surfaced: it wasn't.

They did not meet you there.
They opted out.
And you were left holding the weight alone.
That realization hurts. It tightens the chest, scrambles the mind, and feels deeply personal.

And, paradoxically, it is also clarifying.

Because once the illusion of reciprocity dissolves, freedom returns.

You stop negotiating with chaos.
You stop auditioning for scraps of care.
You stop explaining your worth to people who benefit from misunderstanding you.

Rejection in these moments is not denial—it is redirection. Painful at first. Liberating over time. It reveals a simple truth: Your energy has been invested in the wrong place.

You cannot force someone to show up.
You cannot manufacture accountability.
You cannot will another person into self-awareness.

The only real choice is how long you remain, hoping they will become someone they have already shown you they are not.

When that hope releases, autonomy returns.

Healthy relationships—professional or personal—do not require emotional gymnastics to sustain. They are not riddles to decode.

They feel grounded. Reciprocal. Safe. They steady you rather than drain you.

Unhealthy ones do the opposite.

They demand proof of loyalty.
They reward over-functioning.
They trap you in cycles of explaining, justifying, and self-doubt.

And eventually, they collapse under their own imbalance.

Here is a rule worth keeping:
Never accept feedback about your integrity from someone unwilling to face their own.

Words spoken from avoidance, insecurity, or unhealed ego are not mirrors.They are projections.

Eventually, the mask slips.
The truth surfaces.
And clarity arrives—often disguised as pain.

Your responsibility is not to witness every unraveling.
It is to protect your energy.

To step away before chaos pulls you under.
To guard your attention as the finite, valuable resource it is.

The lesson is simple and exacting: Clarity hurts before it instructs. It shows you where boundaries belong, where emotional labor has been misplaced, and where your presence has been overextended.

Once you accept that someone else's lack of care does not diminish the legitimacy of yours, the power returns—quietly, completely.

You stop chasing the uninvested.
You stop explaining yourself to people committed to misunderstanding you.

You stop waiting for acknowledgment that will never come.

What replaces it is not bitterness.
It is alignment.

And sometimes the most self-respecting move is not confrontation—it is a graceful exit. One that returns you to yourself whole, clear, and unwilling to fund dysfunction again.

The Liberation Line

Where have you been giving more integrity than you receive? Liberation begins the moment you stop waiting for someone to become who they have already shown they are not.

Stop Negotiating with Dysfunction

Every relationship, system, and environment has an intended design. When responsibility, effort, and care are shared as they should be, things move. Work flows. Relationships steady. Life feels lighter.

But when roles become drains instead of sources, something shifts.

What should support you begins to consume you.
What should be reciprocal becomes extractive.
And what you hoped would stabilize instead does the opposite.

At that point, you face a choice:
Continue negotiating with dysfunction—or reclaim your energy.

Stop negotiating with people who benefit from your confusion.

Some dynamics only function when your attention is scattered and your confidence eroded. Every carefully worded email, every over-explained boundary, every attempt to "be reasonable" simply reinforces their position.

Their chaos is not your puzzle to solve.
Their confusion is not your responsibility.

Stop explaining your boundaries to people who repeatedly violate them.

Boundaries are not suggestions. They are standards. They do not require consensus, permission, or understanding to be valid. Trying to convince someone committed to ignoring your limits is like pouring water into a cracked vessel—no matter how much you give, it will never hold.

Alignment begins the moment explanation ends and enforcement begins.

Stop offering emotional labor where there is no intention to reciprocate.

Empathy, attention, and care are finite resources. Some people will consume endlessly without contributing, growing comfortable with your effort while offering none of their own. Endless giving is not generosity—it is self-erasure.

Protecting your energy is not selfish.
It is essential.

Refusing to subsidize dysfunction with your presence is how you reclaim agency. Access to you is not automatic—it is earned. Time, attention, and emotional availability must be met with respect, consistency, and reciprocity.

If someone cannot meet that standard, release them—cleanly, calmly, without spectacle.

Walking away is not failure.
It is strategy.

It is the quiet decision to value peace over proving a point, alignment over argument, clarity over chaos. When you stop negotiating with dysfunction, your energy returns to where it belongs—into work, relationships, and environments that amplify rather than drain you.

This is the real win:
Choosing integrity over entanglement, peace over reactivity, and self-respect over depletion.

Stop Negotiating with Chaos

Where have you been investing effort hoping it would eventually create reciprocity? What boundary, upheld with consistency, would finally restore your center?

The Pivot: From Survival to Strategy

Naming the drain matters.
Recognizing patterns matters.
Setting boundaries matters.

But none of that is the destination.

Those are survival skills—essential, necessary, and often hard won. They stop the bleeding. They protect your nervous system. They give you back enough clarity to breathe again.

Strategy begins when you no longer organize your life around what drains you.

Survival is reactive.
Strategy is deliberate.

Survival asks, *"How do I get through this?"*
Strategy asks, *"What kind of life am I building—and who belongs in it?"*

This is the pivot.

It is the moment you stop managing dysfunction and start designing alignment. The moment your energy is no longer spent bracing, buffering, or explaining—and is instead invested with intention.

Strategic living requires discipline, not drama.
Awareness, not hypervigilance.
Consistency, not confrontation.

You begin to notice earlier.
You step back sooner.
You disengage without guilt.

Tight shoulders, shallow breath, mental fog, irritability—these are no longer nuisances you push through. They are data. Signals that something is extracting more than it gives. Strategy listens early, not after collapse.

Detachment becomes wisdom, not withdrawal.
It is the space that allows you to respond instead of react. To choose instead of endure. To remain grounded while others spin.

You stop explaining yourself to people committed to misunderstanding you.
You stop negotiating standards with those who benefit from your exhaustion.
You stop offering access where there is no reciprocity.

Instead, you model self-regard.

You say what you mean.
You set expectations clearly.
You repeat them without apology.

Over time, your steadiness reshapes the room. Some people rise to meet it. Others quietly fall away. Neither outcome requires force.

This is not cruelty.
It is clarity.

Strategic living also demands selectivity. Not every provocation deserves your attention. Not every tension requires your engagement. Not every emotional tug earns a response. Your time, focus, and emotional presence are assets. You invest them where they compound—not where they leak.

Accountability begins with you.

You hold yourself to the standard you expect. You show up with integrity, follow through consistently, and let others reveal whether they are aligned or merely attached to the benefits of your over-functioning.

There will always be people who attempt to pull you into storms they created. Your power lies in deciding who earns proximity and who remains outside your gates.

This is not about control.
It is about dignity.

It is the refusal to become the emotional janitor for unresolved chaos. The choice to stop surviving other people's dysfunction and start stewarding your own life with intention.

Access to you is a privilege.
Treat it like one.

Protect it.
Enforce it.
And when necessary, walk away—without bitterness, without spectacle, and without apology.

Because mastery is not loud.
It is quiet.
It is consistent.

And it is intentional.

And once you stop organizing your life around what drains you, something remarkable happens:

Your energy clears.
Your presence steadies.
Your influence deepens.

This is where survival ends—and authorship begins.

What comes next is not about boundaries or protection.

It is about who you become when your energy is finally your own.

The Shift Towards Strategic Living

Clarity Is Not Confrontation

Where has confusion been quietly draining your energy?
What truth are you ready to name—without
softening it for someone else's comfort? Seeking clarity
is not an attack. It is a return to yourself.

Strength in Selectivity

Which relationships, environments, or expectations no
longer deserve the emotional access you once gave freely?
Your energy is sacred.
Choose where it flows—with intention.

The Quiet Reclaiming

Where have you dimmed your presence to keep the peace?
What daily practice will help you stay steady before anyone
else has the chance to pull you off center?
Freedom begins when you stop reacting to dysfunction
and start designing your life from alignment.

Chapter 13:
Your Daily Armor - Habits, Tools, and Sanity-Saving Practices

Habits That Hold You Up

Tools only work if you actually use them. A journal cannot teach self-reflection if it is buried under junk mail. A mindfulness app cannot calm your mind if it never makes it past your phone's home screen. Even the most elegant, science-backed technique is useless if it stays theoretical—admired, bookmarked, and untouched.

What matters is not just knowing what helps—it is building friction-less access to it. The habit that works is the one that fits into the life you are actually living, not the one that looks impressive in someone else's morning routine.

Not every tool in this chapter (or in this book) will resonate, and that is not a failure of discipline. It is discernment. The world is full of people who swear by 5 a.m. ice baths, color-coded planners, or journaling in perfect cursive. If that sounds like medieval punish-ment or a Pinterest hostage situation, let it go. Growth is not about performing self-control; it is about cultivating self-support.

Think of this chapter as a buffet, not a prescription. A few practices that genuinely steady you will outperform a dozen abandoned hacks every time. Consistency beats intensity. Familiar beats flashy.

Smart habits are not about optimizing every minute of your day. They are about reducing unnecessary strain. They are the quiet systems that carry you through deadlines, difficult conversations, traffic jams, and your own overthinking brain. Life does not need more pressure—it needs better support.

Some days will feel less like balance and more like juggling fire, chainsaws, and a crying toddler. In that chaos, habits are not decorative: They are scaffolding. Tiny, repeated acts of intention become emotional muscle memory. You do not need a total life overhaul—you need a few anchors that remind you who you are when everything else is loud.

Earlier work built awareness—learning to notice, name, and understand what was shaping you. Now that awareness has weight. It lives in the small systems that hold your days together and protect what matters.

These practices are not aspirational self-care. They are daily armor—small, deliberate moves that protect your peace, reclaim your focus, and help you show up grounded instead of frayed. One shift at a time. One choice at a time. One breath at a time.

Daily Sanity-Saving Practices

Radical Self-Loyalty

If you spoke to your best friend the way you sometimes talk to yourself, you likely would not have a best friend. Radical self-loyalty means refusing to abandon yourself when things go sideways. It is choosing to stay on your own side when you miss a deadline, say the wrong thing, or spiral into self-doubt.

Self-loyalty does not mean excusing harmful behavior or avoiding accountability. It means correcting without cruelty. It means saying, *"That didn't go well—and I'm still worthy of care."*

Many people mistake self-criticism for responsibility. It is not. It is erosion. Shame does not create growth; safety does. You cannot regulate a nervous system that is constantly under internal attack.

Radical self-loyalty becomes the internal voice that steadies you instead of shaming you. It is the habit of asking, *"What would support me right now?"* instead of *"What's wrong with me?"*

This is a core practice—a foundational habit that sits at the center of this work. It makes everything that follows possible. Without it, habits become punishments. With it, they become support.

Listening like You Mean It

Most people do not listen—they reload. They are waiting to respond, explain, defend, or impress. Real listening is quieter and far rarer. It is attention without an agenda. Presence without performance.

Listening like you care is not passive. It is an active choice to stay with what is being said instead of rushing to resolution. It requires tolerating silence, uncertainty, and emotions that are not yours to fix.

This kind of listening does something powerful: it slows your internal pace. It interrupts mental spirals. It brings your nervous system out of threat mode and into connection. Over time, it also teaches you how to listen to yourself—your body, your intuition, your fatigue—before those signals escalate into burnout.

Listening is not just a relational skill.
It is a regulation strategy.

Emotional Regulation

Emotional regulation is not suppressing feelings or "being calm" at all costs. It is awareness paired with choice. It is recognizing the surge—anger, fear, embarrassment, grief—and deciding how you will move through it.

Regulation gives you a pause. Not a long one. Just enough space to choose whether you want to escalate, disengage, or respond with clarity. That pause is everything.

Without regulation, other people dictate your emotional weather. With it, you remain responsive without being hijacked. You still feel deeply—you just no longer hemorrhage energy reacting to every stimulus.

Regulation is what allows boundaries to be enforced calmly, values to be upheld under pressure, and relationships to be navigated without self-abandonment. It is not about control—it is about agency.

Values and Trust

When life gets messy, and you know it will, your values are what keep you oriented. They are not motivational slogans or abstract ideals. They are the standards you return to when emotions are high and clarity feels distant. It's your values that you always have, no matter what, and you need to come back to them with intention often.

Repeatedly betraying your values to keep the peace costs more than conflict ever will. It creates resentment, confusion, and internal fracture. Alignment, on the other hand, creates coherence. Decisions become cleaner. Boundaries feel less defensive and more declarative.

Trust, whether with yourself or others, is always built the same way: behavior over time, promises kept, follow-through honored, and repair made when necessary. When words and actions align, trust compounds quietly. When they don't, no amount of explanation restores it.

Your Energy Ecosystem

These practices do not operate in isolation. They form an ecosystem.

Your environment, your work, and your relationships are not separate lanes—they are interdependent systems, constantly influencing one another. When one area is neglected, the strain does not stay contained. It shows up somewhere else—usually in your energy, your patience, or your health.

You do not run out of resilience because you are weak.
You run out because too many systems are leaking at once.

Looking at your life through the lenses of environment, work, and relationships reveals where pressure is quietly accumulating. When you understand your life as an ecosystem, you stop defaulting to brute-force fixes. You intervene earlier. You adjust more gently. You recover faster. And instead of pushing harder, you learn where support is actually needed.

Health, Energy, and Rest

You cannot out-discipline biology. Sleep deprivation, chronic dehydration, and sustained stress will override even the strongest mindset. Emotional regulation, focus, and patience all require a body that is not constantly depleted.

Rest is not something you earn after productivity.
It is what makes productivity sustainable.

Joy works the same way. Laughter, play, and rest are not rewards—they are regulators. Burnout is not proof of dedication. It is feedback.

Home as Your Launchpad

Your living space is not just a backdrop—it is a regulator. Clutter, harsh lighting, and constant noise quietly tax your nervous system. An environment that restores you creates calm, supports focus, and sustains creativity. One clear corner, softer light, or an intentional workspace sends a powerful signal: You are safe here.

Ask yourself honestly—does my environment refill me, or drain me drop by drop?

Work as an Energy Multiplier

Work occupies a massive portion of your emotional landscape. Alignment matters. The people you collaborate with either fuel or drain you. The work itself either challenges you meaningfully or buries you in motion without purpose.

Misalignment never stays contained. It spills into your health, your relationships, and your self-worth. Growth is not always upward. Sometimes it is deeper, sharper, or redirected toward meaning rather than metrics.

Relationships as Mirrors

Relationships amplify energy. Some leave you clearer, steadier, and more yourself. Others leave you depleted, doubtful, or emotionally muted. Healthy relationships expand capacity. Toxic ones shrink it. You build off one another's emotions and those emotions are contagious (Boyatzis, et. al., 2013), so be careful.

Like work and environment, relationships require intention and boundaries. They reflect who you are, what you value, and how well your energy is respected.

Small Rituals, Big Impact

Rituals are not about control—they are about containment. They give your nervous system predictable touchpoints of safety throughout the day. When life feels chaotic, small rituals restore rhythm.

A soundscape at night.
A song that shifts your mood.
Five minutes of honest reflection.

These are not minor.
They are stabilizers.

Noise: Your Brain's Night-Shift Supervisor

Sound is one of the most underestimated tools for restoring peace. White noise, brown noise, ocean waves, rainfall, or the steady hum of a fan can anchor a restless mind when it insists on replaying every awkward moment the instant you lie down. These soundscapes give your thoughts somewhere to rest and gently tell your nervous system: *That's enough for today.*

Music: Your Emotional Co-Pilot

Music is one of humanity's oldest medicines. It shifts mood, releases tension, and voices truths you have been editing all day. That song—the one that hits in the chest, unlocks tears, or shakes something loose—does not just accompany you. It escorts you through emotion. Music is therapy with a pulse. We should practice this therapy more often than meets the eye.

Shadow Work and Perspective

Shadow work asks you to face the parts of yourself you would rather avoid—the patterns that sabotage, the habits shaped by old wounds, the stories you inherited instead of choosing. It is not glamorous. It is honest, and it is freeing. Naming the shadow reduces its grip.

Perspective is its companion. Gratitude, humor, and reframing interrupt urgency and comparison. Together, perspective and shadow work reclaim energy, sharpen focus, and restore joy—not by pretending everything is fine, but by seeing clearly.

From Armor to Presence: Where Preparation Becomes Lived

All the habits, micro-practices, and boundaries you have built are not simply tools—they are your armor. They protect your energy, sharpen your focus, and reclaim your mental space. But armor alone does not move you forward. Awareness becomes mastery only when it is used.

Each micro-habit you practice, each boundary you uphold, each environment you curate, and each relationship you choose is an act of self-loyalty. These are not abstract concepts; they are lived decisions. Repeated consistently, they reshape your inner landscape—how you think, how you connect, and how you move through the world.

When your home, work, relationships, and habits align, your energy begins to flow with clarity and resilience. You can move through chaos without losing your center. You can engage fully without being consumed. And when things feel off, the work is often smaller than you think: pause before responding instead of reacting, name a limit without overexplaining, or choose not to carry an emotion that does not belong to you.

Misalignment creates leakage—subtle at first, then costly. Alignment, on the other hand, compounds strength, steadiness, and presence. Small, intentional boundaries restore flow faster than force ever will.

This is the bridge from preparation to presence.

Your daily armor is not something you hide behind. It is the foundation you rise from. It allows you to move through the world awake, intentional, and grounded. The shift from protection to participation is subtle but unmistakable. Insight without action remains potential. Action turns awareness into impact.

Every choice becomes practice:
Pausing to check your energy.
Clearing a space.
Choosing who has access.
Holding a boundary.

None of these moments are dramatic. All of them matter. Each one compounds quietly, shaping not just your habits—but your identity.

You are no longer merely surviving.
You are strategizing.

You have built the infrastructure.
You have named the drains.
You have reclaimed your energy.
You have forged habits that sustain rather than deplete.

Now comes the moment to live from them.

What you have practiced here is not about control or correction but creating conditions that support your energy, your boundaries, and your clarity. When habits are rooted in self-loyalty, they become protection. They become a way forward.

The practices you've cultivated are no longer preparation—they are permission. Permission to move forward without bracing. To show up without shrinking. To participate fully in a life that no longer requires constant repair.

This is where consistency becomes momentum.
Where protection becomes confidence.
Where daily armor becomes a life fully lived.

Turn the page.
Show up fully.
Shut up.
Start living.

Daily Armour, Daily Living

Your Next Brave Step

What is one small action you can take this week that turns
awareness into movement? Name it. Claim it.
Follow through. Momentum grows from the
smallest honest commitment.

Energy as Evidence

How will you know you are living in alignment with
the habits you are building? Look toward your energy:
steadier breath, calmer thoughts, clearer decisions. Your
body reports the truth long before your mind catches up.

The Non-Negotiable

Which habit, boundary, or ritual is ready to become non-
negotiable? Let it anchor your days with intention and self-
respect. Your daily armor becomes real the moment
you live it—not just think about it.

Chapter 14:
Final Thoughts — Shut the Hell Up...and Show Up Better

Maybe your next era is not about chasing, proving, or fixing—maybe it is about becoming. Living with purpose. Raising your standards. Letting go of what no longer serves you. Stepping beyond comfort into the unknown, where growth actually lives. This could be the season to focus on what lights you up, recognize your inherent worth without needing validation, deepen your self-awareness, and nurture habits that genuinely empower you.

Solitude becomes sacred, not lonely. Self-care becomes a responsibility, not an indulgence. You take ownership of your journey—celebrating progress over perfection, presence over performance, gratitude over grasping.

And maybe part of this era is finally letting go of regret. If the hurt was real, offer compassion, take responsibility, make amends where appropriate—and then forgive yourself. Live aligned with the lessons you've learned, the way you wish you had back then. The past is unchangeable, but the present? That is where the power lives. It is a credit to your character that you cannot understand why some people cause harm or ignore compassion entirely.

Let's not overcomplicate it. You could read every leadership book ever printed, attend every conference, collect certificates like Pokémon cards—and still fall flat if you do not show up in the simplest, most basic ways. If you are habitually late, interrupt others, dodge accountability, or treat people as extras in the movie of your life, none of the knowledge or credentials matter.

Leadership is not how you perform on a stage; it is how you show up in the moments no one applauds. Presence has weight. Your tone, your timing, the energy you bring—they speak louder than any speech or strategy deck. Leadership shows up in the text you send after someone's hard day, in the way you look up from your phone when a person needs you, and in how you hold space even when you are tired or frustrated.

Kindness is not transactional; it is a reflection of who you are. In a world desperate to harden your heart, staying soft is courage. Keep shining, especially when it is hard—because that is when light is needed most. Be coachable. Be honest. Be on time. Say thank you. Own your mistakes. **Value others—even when there's no audience.**

Practice appreciation without performance. This is leadership in its purest form. It's the difference between someone who talks a good game and someone who actually plays it.

Most leadership moments do not happen in boardrooms. They unfold in kitchen conversations, car rides home, hallway hellos, and everyday interactions that rarely make the highlight reel. How you move through those ordinary moments—especially when no one is keeping score—shapes your character more than any performance review ever could. Your legacy is built quietly, in the small, often inconvenient choices where you decide to be intentional anyway.

And your words? They are either weapons or beacons. Every hallway chat, Zoom meeting, and group text is an opportunity to make someone feel seen—or small. Words linger long after they leave your mouth. The smallest phrases—"I hear you," "I believe in you," "You matter,"—can be lifelines. Use your words to guide people out of the dark, not push them in deeper. The feeling you leave people with becomes the imprint of your impact. Make that memory a good one.

You are, each of you, an ambassador of change. Your words, presence, and emotional energy ripple outward. Speak with intention.

Listen with humility. Show people that decency, kindness, and accountability still exist in this world. It starts with you.

And then—**get fluent in silence.** The impulse to fill every pause with noise is real, but silence is not empty; it is full of answers. The pause between pain and reaction? That is where maturity and truth live. Learn to sit with discomfort without scrambling for distraction. Growth often happens in the moment you *don't* have a ready answer. When you feel the urge to bolt, numb, scroll, or escape—pause instead. The worst that could happen is that you feel something. And you can survive that. You already have.

It is a rare trust to be invited into someone else's pain or healing. Treat that space with reverence. Show up without needing to fix, rescue, or perform. Sometimes the most powerful thing you can say is nothing at all. Being there is enough. Listening is enough. Holding space is a radical act of admiration and love.

While I would love to hand you a checklist for "what's next," the design of your life from here is yours to create. But start by listening to what triggers you and what brings you joy—those places are asking for care. Define your values. Write them down. Check your behavior against them. Tend to your inner landscape gently and consistently. This is the foundation of authenticity.

Begin each day with a flicker of gratitude—even if just for the coffee in your hand. Assume good intentions in others. Most people are not trying to be awful; they are trying to survive. Extend grace. Shift from catastrophizing to neutral. Small steps create momentum.

Practice the daily art of shutting the hell up—not to disappear, but to listen, to reflect, to stop spilling noise into every quiet moment. That is the real gift. That is leadership. That is what people remember.

Be the sanctuary you always wished for. Create spaces where people can be real. A sanctuary isn't free of hardship—it's where we learn to move through it. Offer that kind of energy. And remember: You are replaceable everywhere except at home. That is where your presence is irreplaceable. That is where legacy is built.

Every choice you make—each time you choose patience over frustration, attention over distraction, listening over interrupting—cements your identity as someone people can count on.

You are not powerless. You are not too late. You are not stuck. You are living proof of what is possible when people choose to lead with integrity, connect with empathy, and commit with their whole hearts.

So be that person.
Speak when it matters.
Stand when it's hard.
Shut up when it's time.
And always—*always*—show up better.

MANTRA SUMMARY:
HOW TO SHOW UP BETTER

Be the person your values claim you are. Silence is power—use it to listen, reflect, and respond. Speak only what matters; use your words to connect, not destroy.

Lead with empathy—especially when it is inconvenient or unseen. Show up fully and authentically. Create sanctuary—for yourself, for others, for the moments that matter.

Pay attention to what triggers or excites you. Follow the clues. Name your values. Align your choices with them.

Shut the hell up... and show up better.
The world is already full of noise. Be the difference.

Final Thoughts, from Me to You

If there is one truth I am carrying into the next season of my life, it is this I want the people in my world- the ones I teach, mentor, lead, or simply cross paths with—to know they can come to me when they struggle, stumble, or get it terribly wrong.

No fear.
No shame.
No hesitation.

Love does not disappear when things get difficult.
Support does not vanish when mistakes happen.

I would rather sit with someone in the middle of their mess than have them face it alone, worried about my reaction.

I am not seeking perfection.
I do not believe it exists.

I want trust.
I want honesty.
I want connection.

Most of all, I want the people I love to know this: There is nothing they could do that would make me stop showing up for them. My care is not conditional. My steadiness is not dependent on circumstances. I am here—consistently, wholly, and without withdrawing when life is hard.

This principle—*safety as a love language*—is the heartbeat beneath so much of what I believe. Not soft skills but soul skills. Nervous system-level strength. The kind of power that steadies storms rather than creating them. The kind of grounding that does not need to shout to be heard yet is felt more deeply than any raised voice ever could be.

And if you are reading these final pages, you have touched this work in your own way.

Maybe you recognized yourself in the stories.

Maybe you found language for something you have long felt but never named. Maybe you remembered a truth you misplaced somewhere along the way.

Wherever you land, hold onto this:

There is no single right way to heal, grow, lead, or love. There is only your way—shaped by your history, your values, your resilience, and your becoming.

This book is not an ending.
It is an opening.

An invitation into deeper grounding.
A reminder that gentleness is not weakness.
A call to be a safe place—for yourself first, and then for others.

Because the world does not need more people performing strength. It needs more people practicing it.

Quietly.
Consistently.
Courageously.

So, if you close these pages with even a small shift in how you see yourself, your relationships, or your capacity to grow, then every word was worth writing.

Remember this:

You are not too much.
You never were.

Your softness is not a liability.
Your steadiness is not accidental.
Your story is not finished.

And hope—steady, grounded, unshakeable hope—still lives here.
In you.
Around you.

Between us.
Welcome to the work.
Welcome to the practice.
Welcome to the kind of strength that feels like calm water after a long storm.

And thank you—truly—for allowing me to walk even a small part of this journey with you.

With care,
Corrie Zimerla

Acknowledgments

This book was never a solitary effort, even though much of it was written in quiet moments, late nights, and in between the lived realities of work, family, and becoming. It was shaped, steadied, and strengthened by people who showed up with honesty, patience, and care.

First and foremost, I want to thank **Dr. Philip Cola**—my trusted editor, collaborator, and steady companion throughout this process. This book is better because of you. You read with rigor and heart, challenged me when clarity mattered, protected the soul of the work, and never once tried to dilute its truth. You held the line between polish and authenticity, between refinement and voice. More than edits, you offered presence, perspective, and belief—especially on days when the work felt heavy. I am deeply grateful for your partnership, your friendship, and your unwavering commitment to helping this book become what it needed to be.

To the friends who listened as these chapters took shape—who let me talk things through, read early drafts, asked the hard questions, and reminded me to rest when I forgot—thank you. Your reflections sharpened my thinking and softened my edges in all the right ways.

To the mentors and teachers—formal and informal—who modeled integrity, emotional intelligence, and quiet leadership long before I had language for it: your influence is woven throughout these pages. You showed me that strength does not need spectacle, that presence matters more than position, and that how we treat people is always the point.

To the colleagues and leaders I've worked alongside over the years— thank you for the lessons, both affirming and challenging. You taught me what alignment feels like, what misalignment costs, and why emotional clarity is not optional for sustainable leadership.

To my family—thank you for your patience, your humor, your grounding, and your love. You reminded me that the most important leadership happens at home, in ordinary moments, where presence matters more than productivity.

And finally, to the readers—especially those who see themselves in these pages—thank you for trusting this work enough to sit with it. If you found language for something you've long carried, if you felt seen rather than fixed, if you closed this book feeling steadier instead of louder, then this journey was worth every word.

No book is written alone.
This one, especially.

With gratitude,
Corrie Zimerla

References

Albom, M. (1997). *Tuesdays with Morrie: An old man, a young man, and life's greatest lesson.* Doubleday.

Baumeister, R. F., Bratslavsky, E., Finkenauer, C., & Vohs, K. D. (2001). Bad is stronger than good. *Review of General Psychology, 5*(4), 323–370. https://doi.org/10.1037/1089-2680.5.4.323

Boyatzis, R. E., Smith, M. L., Van Oosten, E., & Woolford, L. (2013). Developing resonant leaders through emotional intelligence, vision, and coaching. *Organizational Dynamics, 42*(1), 17–24. https://doi.org/10.1016/j.orgdyn.2012.12.003

Blumer, H. (1986). *Symbolic interactionism: Perspective and method.* University of California Press. (Original work published 1969)

Cain, S. (2012). *Quiet: The power of introverts in a world that can't stop talking.* Crown Publishing Group.

Carlson, R. (1997). *Don't sweat the small stuff... and it's all small stuff.* Hyperion.

Chapman, G., & Campbell, R. (1997). *The 5 love languages of children.* Northfield Publishing.

Cola, P.A. & Wang, Y. (2022). Discovering Factors that Influence Physician Scientist Success in Academic Medical Centers. Qualitative Health Research, 32 (10), 1433-1446.

Edmondson, A. C. (1999). Psychological safety and learning behavior in work teams. *Administrative Science Quarterly, 44*(2), 350–383. https://doi.org/10.2307/2666999

Forni, P. M. (2012). *The thinking life: How to thrive in the age of distraction*. St. Martin's Publishing Group.

Gruenert, S., & Whitaker, T. (2015). *School culture rewired: How to define, assess, and transform it*. ASCD.

Granneman, J. (2015). *The secret lives of introverts: Inside our hidden world*. TarcherPerigee.

Greene, R. (1998). *The explosive child: A new approach for understanding and parenting easily frustrated, chronically inflexible children*. HarperCollins.

Greene, R. (2008). *Lost at school: Why our kids with behavioral challenges are falling through the cracks and how we can help them*. Scribner.

Greene, R. (2016). *Raising human beings: Creating a collaborative, compassionate, and connected family*. Scribner.

Hesse, H. (1930). *Narcissus and Goldmund*. S. Fischer Verlag.

Johnston, F., McKee, A., & Boyatzis, R. E. (2008). *Becoming a resonant leader*. Harvard Business Press.

Jung, C. G. (1973). *The psychology of the unconscious*. Dvir Co., Ltd. (Original work published 1917)

Kishimi, I., & Koga, F. (2013). *The courage to be disliked: The Japanese phenomenon that shows you how to change your life and achieve real happiness*. Stone Bridge Press.

Kolb, D. A. (1984). *Experiential learning: Experience as the source of learning and development*. Prentice Hall.

Kozak, A. (2019). *The awakened introvert: Practical mindfulness skills to help you maximize your strengths and thrive in a loud and crazy world*. New Harbinger Publications.

Laney, M. O. (2002). *The introvert advantage: How quiet people can thrive in an extrovert world*. Workman Publishing.

Raichle, M. E., MacLeod, A. M., Snyder, A. Z., Powers, W. J., Gusnard, D. A., & Shulman, G. L. (2001). A default mode of brain function. *Proceedings of the National Academy of Sciences, 98*(2), 676–682. https://doi.org/10.1073/pnas.98.2.676

Redfield, J. (1993). *The Celestine prophecy: An adventure.* Warner Books.